CROSSING THE EXPENDABLE LANDSCAPE

CROSSING THE

# EXPENDABLE LANDSCAPE

*Bettina Drew*

8/16/2014

GRAYWOLF
PRESS

SAINT PAUL
MINNESOTA

Publication of this volume is made possible in part by a grant provided
by the Minnesota State Arts Board through an appropriation by the
Minnesota State Legislature, and by a grant from the National Endow-
ment for the Arts. Significant support has also been provided by
Dayton's, Mervyn's, and Target stores through the Dayton Hudson
Foundation, the Bush Foundation, the Andrew W. Mellon Foundation,
the McKnight Foundation, the General Mills Foundation, the St. Paul
Companies, and other generous contributions from foundations,
corporations, and individuals. To these organizations and individuals
we offer our heartfelt thanks.

Special funding for this title was
provided by the Lannan Foundation.

Published by Graywolf Press
2402 University Avenue, Suite 203
Saint Paul, Minnesota 55114
All rights reserved.

www.graywolfpress.org

Published in the United States of America

ISBN 1-55597-279-9

2  4  6  8  9  7  5  3  1
First Graywolf Printing, 1998

Library of Congress Catalog Card Number: 98-84452

Cover Design: A N D
Cover Photograph: Chris Faust, "Strip Mall Façade, Columbus, Ohio," 1995

ACKNOWLEDGMENTS

My thanks to the Dick Goldensohn Fund for Investigative Journalism
for making possible my work on Dallas. "New City" and "Reflections
in a Mirror Skin Building" first appeared in *Boulevard*. "Please Play the
Machines While You Wait" and "In the Red Rock Valley of the Cowboy
Westerns" originally appeared in *Southwest Review*. "Celebration: A
New Kind of American Town" was first published in the *Yale Review*.

# Contents

*For Martine, Johnny, Theresa,*
*and my dear Groner*

CROSSING THE EXPENDABLE LANDSCAPE

## An Unusual Motivation

*Over the past few years, whenever I had money or the in-*
*clination, I set out to explore the late-twentieth-century*
*American landscape. I began this unusual odyssey because*
*the increasingly new built environment made me curious*
*and suspicious, feelings that reached their peak one morn-*
*ing in 1992 when I opened the* New York Times. *Bypassing*
*the Bosnian horror on the right side and finding no engag-*
*ing feature on the left, I scanned the middle column for the*
*national news—and soon let my coffee go cold.*

*The IRS and Federal Reserve were reporting that during*
*the 1980s the wealthiest 1 percent of Americans had in-*
*creased their share of the country's private net worth from*
*31 percent to 39 percent; the rest of us lost approximately*
*what the richest had gained. Coming much closer to a con-*
*trolling interest in the economy, this 1 percent now owned*
*49 percent of all publicly traded stock, 62 percent of all busi-*
*ness assets, 78 percent of all bonds and trusts, and 45*
*percent of nonresidential real estate. This was the first sig-*
*nificant rise in wealth concentration since the 1920s, what*
*an MIT economist called "an unprecedented jump in in-*
*equality to Great Gatsby levels."*

*I had, of course, suspected something of the kind. We'd*
*seen a class of tramps and a building boom, the same as*
*when wealth moved up in the 1880s and the 1920s.*

*A decade earlier there had hardly been any homeless*
*people in my northern Manhattan neighborhood of Inwood*
*except Dave, a tiny, mentally damaged man who lived in*
*Inwood Park and danced to a strange and secret music when*
*he walked on Broadway, hands to his ears to shut out the*

*world. A few years later, a guy began sitting on the Siamese pipe outside the 207th Street liquor store, panhandling people as they came out happily supplied. Then came the A-train beggars with their rags and missing limbs, and the bundled men who slept in the end-of-the-line subway station on winter nights. Later the women came. There was a small white woman about my age named Annie at the 207th Street station to whom I'd once given my last six dollars and whom I'd briefly glimpsed, weeks later, disappearing amid the sidewalk Christmas trees, still outside.*

*But the homeless were transient, they were excluded, they could apparently be blinked away. The era's buildings offered weighty, material, and more lasting testimony to the reapportionment of wealth.*

*Inwood was too built up to have seen much of the building boom. You could see it in midtown Manhattan, but that had been skyscraper land for so long that the substitution of one tower for another wasn't especially dramatic. The suburbs and outlying lands, however, had been transformed. And just as the 1920s downtown office buildings had dwarfed the red-brick storefronts of the 1880s, so the buildings from the 1980s dwarfed in scope and scale what had gone before. In an age of global dreams, the land had become a showcase for the big-sized everything, the megamarkets and the megamalls and the endless vistas of development housing. Sleek, developer-designed office extravaganzas of reflective glass dotted the suburbs. Malls engineered by marketing experts to control how people moved and behaved and spent had virtually replaced the downtowns of many cities, and much of the American landscape had been turned into a kind of endless commercial. The aesthetic was repetitive and plastic on the roads, where chain food outlets and gas stations and quick-stop marts surrounded nearly every town of size, distracting yet alluring in the protected shopping wonderlands with their beautiful things to see and touch and buy. In the walled-off communities and isolated campuses of corporate headquarters, the feeling was sanitary and impersonal, the watchword security. Everywhere the new rose up to engulf and diminish the past.*

*"The calculation of value in real estate time starts today and looks to the future—the past has no value except as a tax liability," Texas architecture critic Joel Barna has written, and* Edge City *author Joel Garreau was hardly the first to note the excellent profits to be made by building on empty, outlying land. As a result of these realities and of all the highways built for cars, the historic downtowns of American cities have been emptied out and then surrounded by concentric rings of new suburbs. The economic insignificance of the past would explain why developers' representations of that past—in the cutesy signs and bits of re-created architecture in the malls, theme parks, and housing developments—are frequently diminished caricatures that border on contempt.*

*Naturally these caricatures offended me; I remembered George Orwell's warnings about the suppression and manipulation of history, and that past we continually retreat into seemed to me inseparable from life. "Children," Neil Postman once wrote, "are the living messages we send to a time we will not see"; all great buildings, great art, and great literature are about leaving evidence of human tenure, and the possibilities of humanness, on this planet. These things suggest a vision of life as something greater than ourselves. But the world I saw being constructed suggested a very narrow vision indeed. I knew a lot of those great public libraries and parks and promenades from the turn of the century had been gifts from guilt-ridden millionaires in the days before income taxes, but at least they were architectures that suggested the public had something to do with their leisure time*

5

besides spend money. It seemed to me that the increasing orientation of our visual and built reality toward marketing made us attuned to the rationally essential rather than the humanly sustaining; helping to promote the idea of the bottom line as the rationale for just about everything, those strip-commercial landscapes revealed a nation ruled by economic forces with little vision beyond the dollar.

I would have liked to live in a world where past effort actually mattered; I even found the disregard for that effort socially self-destructive. Of course I was resigned to the pervasive role of fantasy in America—the insistence on instant riches and heroic pasts and all that Lewis Lapham has called "the dreaming optimism of the American mind, its delight in metaphor, and its wish to believe in what isn't there." But I'm an American, and I'd learned to live with my big dynamic country's strange proclivities. Still, after reading about the upward movement of wealth, after my part-time teaching colleagues only shrugged cynically when I mentioned it, after it had faded almost immediately from the headlines, I became fascinated with the way Americans had reacted to the shifting of the social structure's huge tectonic plates. As the ideal life had become more elusive, Americans had tripled the amount of money they spent gambling in casinos trying to attain it. As the built past disappeared and buildings were predicated on parking places, people flocked to re-creations of it in the walking worlds of vacation theme parks. As the country became more racially diverse, white people bought houses in gate-guarded communities that, like the old frontier forts, kept the barbarians outside the walls. As CEOS came to earn 190 times the average worker's salary, up from forty times that salary twenty years before, Americans responded with a lack of outrage that suggested they had already suspected it. But what struck me more than anything was the nondiscussion of the *inescapable corporate presence, not only in the world of manufactured goods, but in our very physical built reality and landscape.*

*I sensed that the era's new building might represent a kind of infrastructure for the future, revelatory not only of how marketing experts viewed ordinary Americans but also of the lives we might be expected to lead in the global age. I began my explorations close to home.*

# New City

Dating from the 1600s and known officially as U.S. 1,
the Boston Post Road is the country's oldest continu-
ous route, used by stagecoaches and horsemen who
carried the mail for the colonies. Originating in New
York, it ran past my high school in Mamaroneck all
the way to Boston, and seemed, in my childhood, a
living and inseparable part of the whole concept of
New England. Today the only place where the Boston
Post Road is disrupted is in Stamford, Connecticut,
where it lies buried beneath an enormous shopping
mall. But then, this city of a hundred thousand endured the bizarre experience of demolishing practically everything in its downtown in the late 1960s
and early 1970s. I was meeting a planning official in a
bright new, glossy-white high-rise there, and after I
had passed front-desk security, received my ID badge,
and asked a guard monitoring six or ten closed-circuit
TVs if I was parked in the right place, I began to
understand why the place was called the Stamford
Government Center. It was no city hall from the era
when such buildings expressed a majestic sense of
civic purpose. Bought from GTE moments before the
1980s real estate market collapsed and almost immediately worth millions less than the citizens paid for it,
the government center is corporate, rational, pastless,
and obsessed with security, and I came to see it as the
perfect metaphor for what had happened to the city.
I looked out an upper-floor window to the sterile
pedestrianless canyon of Tresser Boulevard, lined with

awesome and immense glass office buildings that
gleamed with a no-nonsense brilliance in the blue
morning cold. It looked like somebody had dumped
about a billion dollars there.

In 1640 the Atlantic coastal lands on which Stamford
was built were bought for four fathom of wampum
and several dozen hoes, hatchets, coats, kettles,
glasses, and knives; and after a few requisite skir-
mishes with the parties dissatisfied with the deal, the
English exiles who settled there began a relatively homogeneous harbor village that lasted some two hundred years until the railroad came. Then the factories
arrived, making carriages and camphor wax and
shoes; and soon the Irish were cramming themselves
into newly constructed tenement enclaves. Bigotry
followed. Hungry and landless, these non-Yankee,
non-Protestant, and non-English immigrants represented the first major disruption in class the place had
seen. Fortunately, a portrait painter named Linus Yale,
inventor of a pin-tumbler lock with a small flat key,
joined forces with an entrepreneur named Henry R.
Towne, and as their Yale and Towne Lock Company
needed both Stamford's Yankee craftsmen and un-
skilled Irish labor, order and industrialization arrived.
   Farmers and fishermen went under when purvey-
ors of manufactured goods and a professional class of
salesmen emerged; banks were founded, and lawyers
moved in. The majority of males earned wages, however, and as the classes stratified, tramps appeared,
briefly breaking stone before being sent off to prison.
Downtown businesses built red-brick buildings with
plate-glass windows; there was an elegant town hall
and a central park flanked by stylish houses. Infectious

diseases flourished among the Irish, but Yale and Towne was developing into a massive brick, smoke-stacked complex that would employ one out of sixteen people in Stamford. Although civic-minded, Towne liked power. He worked hard to buy out or merge competitors he couldn't reach through patent controls, and despite workers' hands and fingers and arms lost to the machinery in his factory, he locked the place up when twenty-eight craftsmen demanded improvements. In the end the workers had to petition him to reopen and were made to sign an antistrike contract in order to work again.

The sense of itself as dependent on controlling business interests was central to the town's identity as the twentieth century opened. "It would be a hard matter indeed to find a man who does not carry at least one key that is marked made in Stamford, Connecticut, USA," the Board of Trade was boasting by 1925, and the world-famous "Blick" portable Blickensderfer typewriter was made there, along with pianos and chocolates and Milk of Magnesia and an ill-fated car called the Stamobile. Tall brick office buildings appeared in the downtown crossed by trolley lines, and the ease with which the town could switch from making post office boxes to grenades allowed the city to survive two world wars and the Great Depression. But by the late 1940s, the forces set to eradicate the Lock City's past were already in place. Yale and Towne's workers struck, this time successfully, and within two years the company started leaving in a departure so unthinkable people still talk about it. Schick Dry Shavers followed amid a mass exodus of manufacturers seeking cheaper labor. Meanwhile, European war refugees and African

Americans completing their postwar migration northward swelled the population and moved into the tenements of the Irish. But there was no major employer
to absorb the new poor, and the downtown declined.
Curiously, however, outlying farmlands in the surrounding Town of Stamford had been attracting affluent New Yorkers and celebrities like Benny Goodman
and Leopold Stokowski since the advent of the car.
And despite controversy, it seemed inevitable that the
Town and City should consolidate in 1949, bringing
the City under tighter scrutiny and the influence of
the landed gentry. That same year, under the Fair
Housing Act, Congress appropriated the funds for urban renewal that would deliver most of Stamford's
blue-collar past to the wrecking ball.

The federal urban renewal program targeted slums to
be renewed, bought the properties through eminent
domain, demolished them to clear the land, improved
the infrastructure, and sold it—usually at 30 percent of
the cost of all this—to private developers who would
rebuild it in accordance with a preapproved plan. It
was an ends-justified-the-means idea, a product of the
Cold War and the era of the lobotomy, a time of brutal
pragmatism in which deviance was best thought surgi-
cally removed. A program in the American grain,
urban renewal subjugated existing structures, social
values, and ways of life to sweeping, ambitious plans
on which great capitalist fortunes rose and fell. And
just as it is easier to make prisons and alarms and surveillance systems than to understand and prevent
crime, so the essentially mechanistic processes of urban renewal let people avoid understanding that society refused to enforce codes, allowed slumlords to

prosper, and endorsed social segregations that made
blight inevitable. Renewal suggested that slums sprang
not from the American way of life but from the very
buildings themselves, and if the solution in the West
was to move and start elsewhere when the present reality became too ugly, in Eastern cities, where land was
scarcer, the solution was to clear it and try again.

After an earlier six-acre industrial project had been
completed, the Urban Renewal Commission (URC)
that had been established along federal guidelines set
a sixty-six-acre downtown parcel called the Southeast
Quadrant as its priority. The most run-down part of
the city, it hadn't attracted new businesses in a long
time; many stores were empty and apartments abandoned. A newspaper insert endorsing redevelopment
claimed that 94 percent of the housing in the quadrant was substandard, and some of the older wooden
tenements were appalling. Some still had outdoor
plumbing, dangerous heating and electrical arrangements, and bug and rat infestations. That parts of
the quadrant flooded was also cited, with a dramatic
photo, as a reason for the project, although this would
shortly be solved by hurricane barriers that had nothing to do with renewal. Another photo showed an un-
appealing bunch of junked automobiles hogging the
backyards of houses—but the houses themselves
looked decent enough. I had seen other photos from
the renewal area, one in which two old black men sat
on lawn chairs outside a secondhand store, and I had
looked at them in a former redevelopment official's
spacious living room in the Town of Stamford in the
state with the highest income per capita in the country. I knew Larchmont and Mamaroneck and Rye and

Greenwich and the other wealthy Westchester and lower Fairfield County towns along the railroad line to Stamford, knew that junkyards and idle black men served as some of the more potent stereotypes for their residents' seemingly immutable class and racial prejudices. I did not think it was a coincidence that urban renewal became attractive just as black people arrived and the affluent gained political power. The sense of something amiss was later confirmed, and it wasn't just because the newspaper insert was really an ad for renewal rather than a balanced assessment of things. The trouble was that the urban renewal plan in Stamford, promoted as a way to provide "safe, decent, and sanitary housing," wasn't really about housing, and the Southeast Quadrant was only half the story.

"It was old," shrugged a deli counterman who had hung photos of the predemolished Stamford in his shop, his eyes wandering outside to a massive office building housing Fidelity Investments. "It had more character." Stamford had had a three-story brick downtown where trolleys and later buses stopped at the war memorial; it had a school. Old atlases labeling Turner's Garage and the Murphy five-and-ten and hundreds of other tiny shops reveal a way of life made up of individuals and human-scale buildings, a world entirely removed from the huge corporate structures that today occupy the land. "To me, coming from New York, Stamford was a Shangri-La," said a man who opened a furniture store in the downtown in 1954. "It had a bit of everything. There were bakeries and delis and fabric shops and paint stores, even a live chicken shop. Most everything was family operated. We were pleased with the three-story buildings—but you don't look at the building—you see the shoemaker, he has a place, a name. Our kids would shop at the shoe store and sign their name for a pair of sneakers. Was it dirty? No. It was a lot of wonderful people running businesses. We bought a house here. My furniture store was at 508 Main Street and it supported us. We weren't wealthy, but it didn't matter. The wealth was in the living, in being a part of the Stamford community."

Although very run-down at one end, long-gone Pacific Street was a kind of Lower East Side mix of Jewish and Italian merchants and Poles and African Americans, a place whose ethnic intermingling was exemplified by a store called Levine's Italian Grocery. "There was a good secondhand bookstore in downtown Stamford and I felt comfortable there," recalled an artist who later became active in preservation. A number of shops had done business in the same location for fifty or eighty or a hundred years. There was a block of Brooklyn-type brownstones on Bell Street and a row of Greek Revival houses on Cottage, Victorian and workers' row houses, a gas station in the stone carriage house of an old mansion. In this warren of small streets, Canal followed the line of an old waterway long since filled; Stage still had, before the wrecking ball, liveries and a blacksmith's shop with all the old tools. On one corner there was a turreted former bank and a statuesque 1920s office building that were demolished to improve traffic flow but whose locations are now a rarely visited grass-covered lot called a park.

However reluctantly, by the early 1960s the public began to accept the idea that parts of the downtown would be redeveloped. Ten years before, Interstate 95 had displaced some one thousand downtown families; the sixty-six-acre project clearing junkyards and a number of homes had been completed; and wrecking and bulldozing for progress were in the language of the day. And because a New York federal housing official recommended it to a URC member with little background in real estate or planning, Stamford was one of the few cities to use the "preselected sponsor approach" of a single developer. From ten others, the URC picked the team of the developer Pierre Bonan and a local contracting firm named the F. D. Rich Company. Bonan later dropped out, and as Henry Towne had once directed the town, so now would the F. D. Rich Company. A former URC official noted that Stamford was the only town he knew of that had given such power to a single redeveloper. As Robert Rich put it to me, "I bought the downtown."

Victor Gruen Associates, well-known planners who favored wide streets and superblocks, devised new traffic arteries and parking and a pedestrian mall, but Gruen, working to resurrect what was called "a dying body," would reportedly be able to "pump no life" into the downtown without an inner loop highway that would double the renewal project to some 130 acres. Incredibly, the URC easily agreed. The new area across Main Street was primarily nonresidential and could not be justified as slum clearance, but Stamford's urban renewal project, now comprising 80–90 percent of the central business district, became one of the most radical in the nation.

"I was serving on the Stamford Community Council, and everyone was excited about the prospect of something being done to revitalize the city," the owner of a small business recalled. "I understood urban renewal to be about housing, about taking people out of slums and putting them into safe, decent, and sanitary housing. But when the Stamford plan was first presented, I understood it to be economic."

Which it was. There was no real intention to concentrate housing in downtown Stamford after renewal. The idea was to establish businesses, cultural outlets, and restaurants and to make the downtown generate more money. Tax revenues had been falling off, and although most of the wealth was now in the suburbs, it was felt that the downtown should carry the tax burden. "Since World War I there had been no market for downtown housing because of the automobile," a former URC official revealingly remarked. "The gentry had moved uptown, and there was no market for downtown housing." Clearly, the people within the renewal area did not constitute a market—a market that would bring an acceptable profit to the developer, that is, since only a small portion of the housing that was built through the federal program was directly subsidized. Gruen's plan did call for 1,200 units of housing—but high-rent and luxury types—and, finally, in response to continued pressure about where the thousand-odd families would be relocated, Rich promised 150 units of moderate-income housing. The other families could be put into the Southfield Village housing project down by the turnpike as space became available; there was a long waiting list, but the displaced would have priority. Thus the project being sold as providing "safe, decent, and sanitary housing" would create only 150 units for the more than one thousand families to be moved out.

The real issue was that some twenty-four million federal dollars would be coming to town, along with

huge private investment sums, and the feeling was
that this influx would help everybody. All the establishment forces—the one newspaper, the one radio
station, the banks, the mayor, the big civic groups—
strongly favored renewal. Black community leaders
fell in with the plan because they thought they were
going to get new housing. A civic group formed to
promote public participation in the project, with an
executive council made up largely of corporate heads
and businessmen, completely favored the plan. Bol-
stered by well-intentioned rhetoric that bore little relation to the proposed result, renewal was supported
by Stamford's liberal Democratic element. But the extreme nature of the project suggests that many of its
supporters hated the downtown so much they wanted
to eradicate it. And however much they abhorred the
term *Negro removal*, which occurs in all the literature
about the federal program, that was a great part of
what they were actually doing. Successful profit-
minded developers do not generally like having poor
people of any color next to their nice new properties,
and probably due to the sheer enormity of their task,
the URC's fate was to become the developer's hand-
maiden. A "rubber stamp," "sold us out," "gave the
developers carte blanche" were expressions I heard
often from residents; "my perception was that while
they may have turned projects down, I don't remember any," a former city planner recalled. "If you included anything in the area that smacked of the lower
classes," the preservationist said, "the developer
would want to tear it down."

In those days before the landmarks law, the URC
asked the historical society if there were any buildings
in that 120 or 130 acres that should be spared. But the

small society, unwilling to engage in a political battle and seeing its function as primarily archival, said no, and that was that. A number of citizens wondered what the URC was doing to keep the destruction to a minimum, but the answer was nothing at all. A preservationist had asked the chairman of the URC if there were nothing that could be saved and was told, referring to a magnificent Beaux Arts structure, "Possibly the Old Town Hall—if you can find a use for it." The people against renewal were fighting a powerful machine, and the most prominent opposition lawyer sensed it from the first. He was upset at the whole concept of moving people out of an area to create a tax base, which he saw as equating people with dollars. "I represented a man who owned a hardware store that had operated out of the same building for 113 years," he recalled. "We listened to why the building would have to come down and we presented the URC with architectural renderings that would allow the building to be changed to conform to what they wanted." The owner offered to cut two stories off the top, extend his store out thirty feet for pedestrian convenience, and resurface the front of his building to blend in with the renewal area. But that wasn't enough for the URC, which tore down almost all the old Park Row stores around Veteran's Plaza, today the entrance to Saks Fifth Avenue in the mall.

In fact, the small businessman, and especially the ethnic businessman, was a main target of the demolition plan. The majority rented their locations and received only moving expenses when they left, knowing that larger stores would be wooed in to replace them in a bald upward and nonlocalized concentration of capital. And the plan did succeed brilliantly in driving the small entrepreneur out of downtown Stamford. Of

the three hundred businesses moved out of the demolished area, only about ten ever moved back in, and of
those only one, the furniture store, survived to close
in the early 1990s.

The lawyer was made to feel like a social outcast.
His suit had been bankrolled by a Rockefeller heir who
had supported ultraconservative John Birch Society
projects in other Connecticut towns, and so the entire
opposition movement, from preservationists to simple
doubters, were labeled John Birchers while the forces
of big development and demolition, who had already
demonstrated an utter lack of interest in affordable
housing or the community-based shop owner, posi-
tioned themselves as forward thinking and progressive. In the end the lawyer's suit forced a review of the
plan to see if it fit federal guidelines, and three apartment towers of about 120 units each—the 360 units of
affordable downtown housing today called St. John's
Towers—came about solely as a result of his efforts.

There was no point investing in them, so the con-
demned buildings deteriorated until the leveling began in earnest around 1968 and continued for some
eight years. Like the number of acres involved or the
families displaced or businesses forced out, the number of lost buildings varied from four hundred to eight
hundred, depending on whom I spoke to, with six
hundred being the most commonly mentioned figure.
That would mean wrecking-ball action every five or
six days for eight years, and it soon looked like a
wasteland, geographically disorienting and weird, the
flattened debris harsh and glaring in black-and-white
photos. "Suddenly it was all around us, buildings being demolished, the insurance companies raising

*19*

rates, and it felt like a war zone," the furniture man recalled. "The downtown looked like ground zero," a lifelong resident remembered; "an atomic bomb approach," said another. "I was serving in Turkey in the military," a veteran recalled, "and when I came home the town was razed." "The city looked bombed," the preservationist shrugged. "The streets were gone and people got lost because there weren't any landmarks anymore." No one wanted to dwell on the subject, and even supporters of renewal winced when I asked what it was like to live in Stamford then. The destruction was universally upsetting, and almost everyone used the language of war, as if no other images could convey it.

In the five or six books on urban renewal I borrowed from a university library in New York, only one contained a chapter about how such destruction affected people psychologically, a study of people relocated from Boston's demolished West End. "For the majority it seems quite precise to speak of their reactions as expressions of grief," the author wrote. About 40 percent of these displaced people felt helpless or ill or just plain angry for more than two years; they spoke in depressive tones, showed frequent symptoms of psychosocial or social or somatic distress, had to work hard to adapt to their new places, and used language that was unambiguous. "I felt as though I had lost everything"; "I felt like my heart was taken out of me"; "I felt like taking the gaspipe"; "I lost all the friends I knew"; "I always felt I had to go home to the West End and even now I feel like crying when I pass by"; "Something of me went with the West End"; "What's the use of thinking about it"; "I felt cheated";

"I threw up a lot"; "I had a nervous breakdown."
When asked about seeing or hearing that the building
they had lived in had been demolished, fully half reported deeply depressed or disturbed reactions.

In Stamford the grief had to have gone beyond the
relocated families, because practically the whole central business district was destroyed, a loss, too, for
those who knew the downtown intimately because
they owned stores or worked there. The city center
was also the point of reference for many other people,
those who shopped there, or who had grown up in
Stamford, people for whom that particular built past
represented, even run down, a sense of continuity,
something dependably there that provided an orientation to the rest of the world. Their feelings could not
really be expressed. There were few outlets since the
media was largely prorenewal; young people were
protesting against the government by 1968, but the
middle-aged business and homeowners in downtown
Stamford weren't so far removed from the era of black-
lists and smeared reputations. Sympathetic shop
owners and friends outside the renewal area told the
lawyer the word was out that violations might be
found on their premises if they supported him. And
in general, opponents to renewal were made to seem
to be opposing progress and the new Stamford. "The
newspaper articles were always suggesting that we
were on the forefront of something, ahead of everyone else," the veteran recalled. "We were going to get
rid of all that old, outmoded stuff and be forward
looking, we were going to have a new, modern city
of glass and steel, a new tax base." And indeed they
were marching toward the future. "The city had one

attorney, who had many other things to attend to,"
a former chairman of the URC recalled, "but Rich's attorney was full time, and he wanted latitude for Rich."
The disposition ended up heavily weighted in favor of
the developer over the city.

Amid the wasted landscape, photographs taken in
1975 reveal the completed housing towers resulting
from the lawsuit, the space-age Landmark Office
Tower that Rich built in a considerable but successful
gamble to suggest the new Stamford, and the inverted
ziggurat of mirror and chrome of the GTE Building,
sitting in the expanse of rubble and thruway as a striking symbol of the new order. Propelled out of New
York City by a bomb attack and fairly frantic about security, GTE designed a self-contained building with its
own cafeteria, health club, and landscaped decks; the
only pedestrian entrance is through a small guarded
vestibule equipped with elaborate monitoring equipment. Rich was successful in marketing Stamford's
empty land to corporations eager to follow GTE's lead,
and the moniker of "Corporate City" took hold. By
the middle of the massive 1980s building boom, the
major corporate headquarters in Stamford outnumbered those in any city but New York and Chicago,
and many of them settled near GTE along Tresser.

Like most corporations that had been seeking suburban peace since the mid-1950s, these companies
wanted to eliminate the distractions of city life and
encourage people to work longer and more productive
hours. Their inwardly turned nature was reflected, architecturally, in their divorce from the street. Tresser
had never been planned for retail, but the new build-

ings had virtually no sidewalk access. Instead, they began three stories up, designed to be seen as statements of corporate wealth for the huge audiences along Interstate 95. The Amenity Bonus Program illustrated how the developers and their clients felt about the citizens of Stamford. Under this plan, developers were awarded extra floor-to-area ratio (FAR) if they granted a public amenity such as an outdoor plaza, community room, or pedestrian access to parking garages. Unfortunately, "the choice of amenities was left solely to the developer, which, in many cases, resulted in technical compliance with the regulations but no substantial benefit to the community," one observer noted. "It would appear from the concealed location of many of the public plazas that the developers consciously endeavored to discourage [their] use . . . despite the fact that this amenity was most often used by developers to earn premium FAR. . . . a glaring example is the General Reinsurance Building's public plaza, which is located well behind its enormous structure, with access via a side road opposite a car dealership and further through an uninviting chain link fence." A number of plazas are hard and sterile and sometimes don't even have furniture; some cannot be reached by emergency vehicles. As for the community rooms, their total advertising, as of 1989, consisted of one 1978 article in the *Stamford Advocate*.

There were never any real restraints on what the buildings would look like. The URC's review board certainly wasn't going to stand in a developer's way, and like many cities, Stamford doesn't have a design review board. To be built, a structure has only to conform to zoning and other codes. Although urban

renewal had been approved by public hearings in the
sixties, after the contracts were signed the URC had
only to bring projects before the planning board and
the city's board of representatives for approval. The
public was no longer directly involved, and over the
years the URC became increasingly estranged even
from municipal government, occupying a separate office at a safe remove from the government offices. The
city planner remembered a meeting when the URC
was seeking approval for several enormous projects
comprising some 1.5 million square feet of office space
and two hundred units. Because of the potentially
tremendous impact on the downtown, the planning
board wanted time to study the plan. But the URC,
with only thirty days to respond to the developer,
pushed for approval. The URC was utterly task oriented, eager to engineer human society with buildings, and while their failure to acknowledge the
human needs of Stamford's citizens bordered on contempt, the URC felt they were accomplishing their
goal—a goal so tremendous that it demanded expedi-
ency. Like the F. D. Rich Company, they had an interest in getting the biggest possible pieces to cover that
empty land.

As if Tresser had not provided enough of the monolithic and impersonal, Rich proposed an enormous enclosed shopping mall to be built on top of the Boston
Post Road, there known as Main Street. "Rich got the
Taubman shopping-center people to come in and do
a mall. They wanted limited access so that everyone
would shop in their stores. If we had said no, they
would have gone away," the head of the URC from
1974 to 1984 said, illustrating the way the URC tended

to operate. With a substantial interest in the venture, Rich claimed that the big department stores would not come unless they were in a mall, and the enterprise was sold to surrounding area businesses as an investment that would have a tremendous spillover effect. That has not occurred. Appropriately called the Stamford Town Center, the mall *is* downtown retail. Described as "a megastructure with concrete ramps shooting out like twisted arms," it's an upscale mall like hundreds throughout the country, and it was used, in fact, as the location for the movie *Scenes from a Mall*. It has Saks and Macy's and Victoria's Secret and the Body Shop and Fendi, and nearly every store in it is a chain, staffed in the main by young hourly workers with no future or ties there. The substitution of the family-owned business for the corporate chain could hardly have been more efficiently engineered. "The public had little or no input in the mall," the city planner stated bluntly. It was handled in the same way as Tresser, despite the fact that some fifteen years had passed since the disposition, that the plan had not included a closed mall, and that much had been learned, in the intervening years, about the effect of malls on surrounding urban areas. But even if the public had wanted to attend the board of representatives meeting about the mall, they wouldn't have been able to participate. The massive, inwardly turned mall was built. Often called "Fort Stamford," it faces Broad Street with a twelve-hundred-foot concrete stretch that has been referred to as "the Great Wall." And to mark the spot where the Boston Post Road went through, there is an enclosed arcade called the Shoppes at Old Main Street, where old-fashioned street lamps and miniaturized, fake architectural details have been placed as a developer's offhand nod to the city's past.

During the nationwide building boom in the 1980s, Greenwich and other nearby towns called for moratoriums on development, but Stamford rushed headlong into the mentality of buy and flip on its way to creating almost six million square feet of office space. Huge reflective glass installations were built on the way to the Shippan peninsula near Long Island Sound; downtown, demolition continued outside the renewal area as real estate speculators, lured by the corporate presence and armed with free-flowing money from banks and savings and loans, flocked to the town that had so admirably demonstrated its eagerness to create those clean and potentially profitable slates of land. Summer Street, once lined with gracious old trees and large Victorian residences, is today a long row of uninspired commercial office boxes perched above now-banned sidewalk-level parking garages. The Victorians came down one after another as the Zoning Board of Appeals kept granting variances. In 1977, a preservationist conducted a community development survey of some twenty-two hundred older downtown properties outside the renewal area, and when it was reviewed again around 1990, about five hundred of them were gone. In the 1980s the preservationist, asking the F. D. Rich Company to save a block of Victorians on Suburban Street, heard the same language used some twenty years earlier: "No, it's a cancer, we have to remove every bit of it." The land was bulldozed and later sold to an offshoot of the Texas megadeveloper Trammell Crow. Then the owner of the Yale and Towne complex, spooked at having one of the largest commercial prop-

erties on the Eastern seaboard listed on the purely hon-
orary National Register of Historic Places, demolished a
million square feet of it. Finally, people came home
from the Christmas holiday in 1984 to find the old
Stamford Armory gone in a quickie wrecking action so
shocking the mayor of this prodevelopment city sponsored a demolition delay order. Several hundred buildings were torn down after its passage, but finally a
change in the 1986 tax law made speculative investments less attractive, the real estate market collapsed,
and the whole frenzy came to a halt. In the meantime,
an estimated 60–70 percent of the housing on periph-
eral downtown streets had been lost, a circumstance
that has continued to force up the price of housing in
Stamford. Where the armory stood, First Stamford
Place, a long and chilling reflective glass complex,
hugs the railroad line as the visitor's first introduction
to the city.

Some years ago, a longtime Stamford resident happened to pass through Watertown, Massachusetts,
with a strange sense of déjà vu. "It reminded me of the
old Stamford. It gave the same impression, of an old
brick city with the new intermixed. That's the only
way I can remember it, to go to another town that
was like it. Otherwise it's no longer in my head. They
wiped it totally out of our consciousness." When I
heard remarks like this or saw the photographs in the
deli or the large mural on Summer Street of old-time
Stamford, painted by a group of residents when the
downtown was a vacant lot and still respected and intact some eighteen years later, I was always shocked at
the way these efforts of ordinary people to express
the idea that the past had been meaningful could not

*27*

begin to compete with the impersonal power of the office buildings.

"After we saw that F. D. Rich was just putting up corporate structures for Fortune 500 companies and that was all there was," after the cries of "no more Manhattanization," after the price of rental housing kept going up and the people who weren't CEOs felt they'd been sold out—"when people realized," as the preservationist put it, "that it wasn't their town any-more"—suddenly people began to join the preserva-tion group: cops, homeowners, all kinds of people. The historical society, too, began to take a more active role in protecting what remained of the town's past. "I know people miss the old town," the preservationist said, "because there is so much 'do you remember?' I meet people all the time and they say, 'Do you remem-ber this building or that old place?'" In the late 1980s, the URC was summing up its achievements at a com-munity meeting and an official was showing slides of the lost downtown. He expected the audience to see how run down it had been and what a great job had been done in getting rid of it. Instead, without any prompting at all, the people began to chant. "Put it back! Put it back! Put it back!"

Amid so many austere buildings, I thought it would be a relief to enter the branch of the Whitney Museum that occupies the street level of the Champion Building on Atlantic Street. I saw three vacuum clean-ers in a display case; a life-size facsimile of five organ pipes, a keyboard and foot pedals that could not be played; selected aphorisms in digital display. I was glad it was there but the sculptures seemed sanitary, uncontroversial, as emotionally barren as the buildings outside. Across the street, the Rich Forum, Stamford's arts center, was one of the last pieces of the downtown to be put into place. Although a low building, it is clean and modern and in keeping with the giants around it, booking ballet and concerts and rather mainstream theater. But at the intersection of Tresser and Atlantic, a corner mostly busy only at lunchtime and when the cars file in and out at the beginning and end of the day, it seems strangely static, its electronic display sign revolving endlessly into the empty street.

For a while after the 1980s building boom, Stamford declined. F. D. Rich lost most of its holdings, and sometimes the vacancy rate for office space reached 24 percent. The corporations that once occupied the buildings were swallowed up in mergers or leveraged buyouts, or, having to downsize, went where their costs were lower. At various times residents have faced projected tax increases that, reflecting these losses, averaged more than 30 percent to maintain the same level of city services. The new Stamford was once known as a financial success and an emotional failure, but even its monetary worth has not proved especially secure. Unlike many cities that renewed, however, Stamford has completed most of its plan and is known as one of the success stories of the program.

To me, Tresser's empty soullessness seemed the realized vision of a 1960s science fiction novel, and though Bob Rich told me I was probably the only person ever to do so, I climbed the gargantuan stairs to the General Reinsurance Company. I was trying to get to the public plaza after having been denied entrance

inside by security guards, and I sensed acutely that in
relation to the enormous building massed above me I
was a creature of little importance. The moonscape of
Tresser is indifferent to the individual. The City's planning office has been trying to humanize it by various
means, and a new generation of URC leadership real-
izes all too well the follies of the past, but what has
been built is too big to be fundamentally changed,
and it offers the citizens of this city who traded their
past for it an enduring presence that is predicated
on the fear of people like themselves.

   "The ideology of the age of globalization celebrates
the liberation from passionate attachments to any specific piece of territory," the authors of a recent study
of global corporations and the new world order have
written, and Stamford's new architecture is in that
spirit, international and indifferent to locality. It is no
accident that once–New England Stamford looks, as
Paul Goldberger has described it, like a Sun Belt city, or
that many of the corporations that left it went to the
far vaster deal-hunting grounds in Dallas. Like much
of the rest of the country, Stamford physically came to
represent the dawning of a new economic era. When
the manufacturing jobs went where the making was
cheaper, the city embraced the corporate presence
with an almost pathetic fervor, not yet aware that the
age in which the great empires were based in specific
places, like Rome or Detroit or Silicon Valley, was
largely over. And there is something else too. The urban sociologist William H. Whyte has noted that
"when building investment is allocated on the basis of
real estate gambles, not community needs, urban ugli-
ness goes deeper than form or surface"; architecture

historian Vincent Scully has observed that a society will build what it values. Based as it was on the idea that the only thing that mattered was a tax base, the design of Stamford reduced its citizens to the bottom line. It was in this way, finally, that Stamford seemed to me most emblematic of the United States today.

# Privatopia

*I had always been curious about all those new gate-guarded
communities. Mostly they are community-interest developments (CIDs), private subdivisions where residents share golf
courses, swimming pools, tennis courts, open space, and
other amenities in common. Organized around a series of
covenants, codes, and restrictions (CC&Rs) that may dictate
what color houses may be painted, where cars may be
parked, where trees may be planted, and other details of daily
life, CIDs are governed by homeowners' associations that enforce these rules. The guiding mission of these associations,
in which all home buyers become members upon signing
their deeds, is to preserve property values, and the communities display an astonishing conformity of appearance.*

*CIDs had their origins in the 1910s, when a man named
Jesse Clyde Nichols, pioneer of the modern shopping center
and a major builder of Kansas City housing, set up a voluntary homeowners' association for his Kansas City Country
Club District development. Unfortunately, the group became too independent for Nichols, so for another project in
1914 he tried a strictly controlled, mandatory association
for which he would write the rules. He bound the association
to enforce these rules and to maintain vacant property, hire
contractors, remove snow, and perform other tasks for the
development's good. But "what a new resident might or
might not have seen," maintained William S. Worley, author of a 1990 study of Nichols, "was that it also had a
benevolent despot in the person of J. C. Nichols who would
make sure everything stayed that way."*

*The idea of deed restrictions caught on, although in the*

*first half of the century* CIDs *were usually built only for the rich. During the middle-class suburbanization of the 1950s, by contrast, developers built on large lots, land then being cheap and the government often building roads and sewers as well as subsidizing mortgages. But then, according to Evan McKenzie, author of* Privatopia, *"the home-building industry, which was by 1960 increasingly dominated by corporate builders . . . could foresee a time when they might no longer be able to build 'big lot' suburban houses at prices the middle class could afford." In 1948, the cost of land developed with roads, water, and sewers made up 11 percent of the price of a new home; this cost rose and rose until by the 1970s it represented some 25 percent to 30 percent. In the mid-1960s Uncle Sam tried to address the land-cost problem by helping to subsidize "new towns" like Reston, Virginia, Irvine, California, and Columbia, Maryland, but gave up when a number of these fell into bankruptcy. More galvanizing, however, was the American Society of Planning Officials' 1960 report on "cluster subdivisions" that proposed CIDs as a solution, one that the Federal Housing Authority heartily approved. "The industry grabbed the idea, and local government accepted it, and FHA insured it, and the concept took off like wildfire," one observer remembered. "These private initiatives in housing policy, and their validation by government, brought about astonishing nationwide growth in CID construction," McKenzie reports. "There were fewer than five hundred such homeowner associations in 1964 . . . by 1992 there were 150,000 associations privately governing an estimated 32 million Americans."*

*CIDs really began to take off in the 1970s, when financially strapped local governments saw in them a way to add property taxpayers to their rolls without substantial investment. And then developers really began to determine the look and feel of communities. In a* CID, *the developer usually writes the* CC&Rs, *as well as the articles of incorporation, bylaws, general rules, and regulations, allowing the creation of distinct lifestyles—for seniors, golfers, singles, or tennis players, for example—that make alluring marketing tools. At first, to ensure control, the developer appoints the association board members and usually retains three votes per unsold unit until all the units are sold. Then the guidelines provide for the election of a board of directors from among the association's membership.*

*But even when residents control the board, these are strange governments for Americans to live under, for they can hardly be said to be democratic. Indeed, legal scholar Adolph Berle, political scientist Grant McConnell, and others assert that private governments like those in corporations, unions, and* CIDs *tend to be oligarchic. In* CIDs, *changes in* CC&Rs *are difficult to bring about because they require a two-thirds or sometimes four-fifths vote of the entire membership rather than a simple majority; renters, who constitute a substantial minority and in some developments a majority, generally cannot vote. When disputes arise as to whether a resident is adhering to a rule, there are no provisions for an impartial jury or judge; most issues are simply brought before the board. Homeowner associations may also restrict the length of a guest's visit, the ages of residents, the number of occupants in the home, and whether any kind of business may be conducted there. Moreover, McKenzie reports, "Most* CID *boards have the right to enter individual homes as they deem appropriate and necessary to protect everyone's investment. The individual is subservient to the corporation, and residents must learn to accept this fact."*

*That so many Americans are willing to live under such conditions in order to protect their property values speaks*

volumes about the economic insecurity of even fairly fortunate people. It also speaks volumes for how willingly people
have given up their democratic rights, and how acceptable
autocratic rule really is to large numbers of Americans.
Moreover, that for so many property values have become the
de facto definition of the social good and that community is
now a product we can purchase, rather than something we
create for ourselves, suggests how deeply the values of the
marketplace have penetrated our domestic lives.

The privatization that has occurred with the rise in CIDs
happened over decades as developers transferred local government functions bit by bit to the private sector. It was
never a conscious decision by the American public or the
subject of mass debate or referendum. While helping to pri-
vatize local government, CID home buyers have been un-
aware of the implications of their actions because the retreat
of so many millions of people from local public government
has never been adequately explored by government or academia. "Developers and other proponents of CIDs typically ar-
gue that people consent to the rules of a CID by buying and
living there," McKenzie has written. "But . . . it is increasingly difficult to find non-CID housing in many parts of the
country . . . [and] as the real estate market consolidates at
the large corporate level, the opportunity for real choice
among CIDs—that is, for meaningful choices among different lifestyles and regimes of rules—may be diminishing.
Any diversity that exists is provided at the discretion of the
real estate development industry."

Former labor secretary Robert Reich has lamented that

> in many cities and towns, the wealthy have in effect with-
> drawn their dollars from the support of public spaces and in-
> stitutions shared by all and dedicated the savings to their
> own private services. . . . The continuing debate over whether
> the wealthy are paying their fair share of taxes obscures a

*larger issue, with more profound implications for America: the fortunate fifth is quietly seceding from the rest of the nation.*

The conservative social scientist Charles Murray has also wondered what will happen as "10 or 20 percent of the population has enough income to bypass the social institutions it doesn't like in ways that only the top fraction of 1 percent used to be able to do," and he fears that this population "will come to view cities as the internal equivalent of Indian reservations—places of deprivation and dysfunction for which they have no responsibility." In CIDs an "I've got mine" mentality allows residents who are satisfied with their own situation to push to the edges of their consciousness the idea that citizens, whatever their differences, are connected to a civic whole that is greater than themselves.

Industry estimates suggest that by the year 2000 the number of homeowner associations will grow to 225,000, raising the specter that some forty-eight million Americans will be living under CID governments. This was why I thought Hilton Head, South Carolina, an island developed almost entirely with CID housing, might be a useful place to explore.

## The Coastal Empire

When I think of Hilton Head Island, the first scene
I remember is an empty winter beach at low tide, the
sky just cleared after a midday rain. The misty bright-
ness was so diffuse the beach seemed a planet of light
and the thousandfold roaring of the inside of a shell;
shielding my eyes, I could make out a jagged line of
seagulls standing on the gray-beige expanse of a
would-be sandbar, puffs of clouds behind them
over the distant and tumbling foam. Here was the
Atlantic's New England rawness, the sea smell and the
metal-colored ocean and the scraggy dune grasses, and
with it the kind weather, fine sand, and palmlike trees
of the tropics. What intelligent developer could have
resisted it? And a sign stuck in the dunes of "Marriott's
Grand Ocean—Models Open" reminded me that very
few had.

The second scene happens every early morning
and late afternoon at a place known locally as the
Courthouse Annex on Route 278, the road leading
onto the island from the bridge to the mainland. The
Annex itself no longer exists, but the buses of the
Lowcountry Regional Transit Authority stop in the lot
where it once stood. I'd seen a couple of LRTA buses
before, dusty old Blue Birds that reminded me of the
segregated South and looked utterly out of place on
the corporately manicured island with its expensive
cars. The buses at the Annex, however, seemed re-
conditioned. On the afternoon I watched them, the
people who clean the rooms and tend the gardens of

Hilton Head got off buses from the places where they worked and waited to transfer to others that would take them to homes up to two hours away. They wore sweat suits and jeans and sneakers and comfortable shoes; most carried a backpack or shoulder bag that probably contained a uniform. Some hung around on the unpaved lot and smoked cigarettes; portly bus drivers alighted to stretch their legs. "Some of them need to make up fourteen rooms before they punch out at four," the voice of a labor organizer I'd interviewed played over in my mind; these workers earn between five and seven dollars an hour, and on some days landscapers make the two-hour commute, find it raining on the island, and have to go home without pay. I saw a light-skinned woman and wondered for a moment whether she might be Latina or Native American. But as she boarded her bus I saw her more clearly. "It's our own little South Africa right here," the town councilman had described it. Every person on the buses was black.

This was most definitely South Carolina.

Fringed almost entirely by fabulous beaches, Hilton Head is a resort and retirement community that prides itself on an image of wealth so carefully honed that a call to the chamber of commerce put me in touch with a New York PR firm. The island is made up for the most part of large community-interest developments, which, along with their miles of private beachfront, offer homes, vacation villas, marinas, restaurants, shops, and recreational amenities. These properties, called *plantations*, are private and have manned entrance gates. Sometimes, when neither my book contract nor my university affiliation was enough to

wangle even a drive through one of these essentially
predictable developments, I wondered what those
gates were really about. But my irritation was usually
assuaged by evening, after I'd returned to my hotel.
I had chosen it over the phone because of its indoor
pool and low winter rates, and I'd expected a motel on
a noisy commercial strip. Instead, it was calm and
pleasant and tucked away, a time-share community
that rented rooms in the off-season, and it made me
understand why most visitors come to the island to
rest. My room overlooked a shallow man-made lagoon,
and I enjoyed the wide path cleared for me by the
dozen or so resident ducks who quacked a low but distinct disapproval whenever I passed.

But mostly Hilton Head seemed about driving a
new silver rental car up and down Route 278, the long
ten-mile or so William Hilton Parkway that runs down
the center of the island. There's so little public access
to the beaches that the parkway is, in a curious way,
Hilton Head's only significant public domain. Unlike
other American islands, Hilton Head has no town in
the sense that the word is generally understood. It has
no center.

There's almost no strip commercial on 278. There's
some development entering from the mainland, but
soon the road passes luxuriant and undulating golf
courses flanked by palmetto and pine trees; the medi-
ans are all cut grass and well-kept shrubs, and at the
infrequent stoplights the entrances to plantations are
marked by tasteful earth-toned signs. The whole effect
is restful on the eyes, except for the glare of speeding
metal and machine-perfected asphalt. And all the
ingredients for modern life are here, the Wal-Mart,

supermarkets, and malls set far back from the road to
meet the island's stringent zoning codes. In many
ways the development suggests the forefront of tasteful planning, but that it is all predicated on the car
gives a strange sense of elongation and distance and
isolation that speaks of nothing if not the late twentieth century. The vast majority of the island's architecture is what is known as "contemporary," and Hilton
Head's visual narrative is deeply about the present.

Route 278 leads right into Sea Pines, which began
in 1956 as the island's first large-scale development.
When its twenty-six-year-old Yale-educated developer
designed the Sea Pines Plantation, he wanted to preserve the island's natural beauty and avoid the standard American beach development, which he saw as a
"hodge-podge of conflicting uses, a joy . . . to all ma-
niac builders and hot dog stand operators, but a nightmare to anyone with reasonable aesthetic standards."
His resort would set off the island's coastline and vegetation with attractive housing, boat harbors, tennis
courts, and golf courses. And in general, the houses of
Sea Pines are delightfully shaded and cozily nestled
into their surroundings, reached by streets that curve
languorously through carefully kept pines. The developer's emphasis on creating a "high-quality destination resort" marketed primarily to the affluent was
central to the island's later identity. In its first decade,
Sea Pines sold homes to more than thirty millionaires,
and by 1973 the incomes of Sea Pines owners were 57
percent higher than the national average.

Almost every major development on the island
has borrowed heavily from Sea Pines—except insofar
as the word *plantation* is concerned. After various

management shuffles, the word was tastefully dropped in favor of simply calling the development Sea Pines. The African American employee driving me around thought this was a good idea. The word *plantation*, he felt, had certain reverberations for some whites, who had seemed to expect service with an inappropriate deference. We took a few moments to see the ruins of an eighteenth-century plantation house on the property, its thick walls made of oyster shells covered with a stucco-like finish called tabby. A plaque dated the house, and plaques beside the foundations of outbuildings identified them as "kitchen" or "storehouse." My guide evinced a certain awe and wonder looking at them, and we were both disappointed that management had seen these one-word signs as adequate.

He also showed me a tiny cemetery next to a group of condominiums in Sea Pine's Harbour Town. Some of the headstones were amazingly simple: a flat stone with the initials W. S. carved in by hand, a smaller stone with no writing at all. Many dated from the 1800s and early 1900s, but two large, professionally carved stones were from 1994. Following an African American custom of calling small sons Master, one marked the place of Master Kareem, aged two. Beside him lay his mother, who had died six months later, still in her twenties. Only a few years ago people had held services in this small graveyard no larger than a spacious room; just in from the sea, it had obviously been chosen as a pretty spot for a resting place.

That little cemetery, surrounded by one of the more ambitious developments in recent memory, one that each summer hosts tennis championships bringing in tens of millions of dollars, was to remind me, later, of certain extreme aspects of life on Hilton Head Island.

But at first it seemed to suggest that despite its over-whelming modernity, the island did indeed have a history, one that I found both cyclical and instructive.

Over the past five hundred years, Hilton Head has been alternately controlled by people who farmed, hunted, fished, and basically left the island as they found it, and those who saw in it the means to large-scale capitalist fortunes. In the 1300s Amerindians were living off the island's plenty and traveling to other islands in dugout canoes to trade. There's some dispute as to their tribe, but they enjoyed a keen appetite for oysters, the shells of which they flung over their shoulders so habitually that borders of shells encircled their villages—the famous Indian "shell rings" of which there are only some twenty-one in the United States. Not just handy garbage dumps, the shell rings formed natural barriers that probably made quite a crunch if intruders tried to cross them in the night.

And of course intruders did come. Spanish adventurers checked in around 1521. Although they were already forcing slaves to grow sugar in the Canary and Cape Verde and Madeira islands, and although Columbus had shipped more than three hundred thirty New World Indians home for the Seville slave markets and as personal gifts, the Spanish were concentrating their kidnap-and-plunder efforts farther south. Apparently they used the island only as a rest stop, drawing water from its wells and feasting on its seafood and wild animals before the long sails home. French Huguenots seeking religious freedom attempted a settlement in the 1560s, but they hardly survived the year. Meanwhile, the Spanish founded

nearby Port Royal, but had to abandon it in the late
1500s as a result of Indian attacks and increasing
British naval power. Indeed, it was the British under
William Hilton who first settled the island in earnest
in the mid-1660s.

These Britons who first settled South Carolina were
not explorers. They were adventuring refugees from
Barbados, the crown colony legendary both for its un-
believably profitable sugar crops and for its cruelty toward the African slaves who produced them. By 1660
Barbados had become so top heavy with the rich and
its land prices so inflated that whites without much
capital could find little opportunity. A few prescient
colonists had petitioned King Charles II to begin a
new colony in South Carolina, where the prized com-
modity of land was plentiful and easy to obtain. Pre-
figuring the yeomen and sons of Southern planters
who would later migrate west to Louisiana and Texas
and the rest of the New South to spread plantation
slavery, the first Barbadians who left for South
Carolina brought along servants and Negroes and
cherished the dream of slave plantations.

Their schemes did not materialize overnight, but
by the early eighteenth century, with the Native
Americans either killed, enslaved, conquered in the
Yamasee War, reduced by European diseases, hunted
to extinction, or simply pushed west, planters ordered
their slaves to plant indigo, the dye whose processing
could cause blood poisoning, and rice, which only became a profitable crop after slaves from African rice-
growing areas brought their expertise to bear. Thanks
to a steady slave trade through Charleston, blacks
early on outnumbered whites in South Carolina. State
politics were dominated by planters, however, and the

state was one of the most rabidly proslavery in the South, its devastating slave code descended directly from Barbados. And South Carolina was, of course, the first state to secede from the Union, its soldiers starting the Civil War by firing upon Fort Sumter in Charleston harbor.

Early in that war, Union strategy was to blockade the coastal Confederacy by sea and then to attack in the Deep South, and in the fall of 1861, Union forces quickly occupied Hilton Head as planters fled the area. Not surprisingly, many local blacks, joined by others from liberated islands nearby, stayed with the army, and Hilton Head became a supply station for Union forces. President Lincoln is said to have freed the Sea Island slaves as early as April 1862, and in September General Ormsby Mitchel set aside a spot on the old Drayton plantation for "a Negro Village," making Hilton Head the site of the first freedmen's village in the United States.

Mitchelville came to include some fifteen hundred souls who worked for wages on the plantations where they had been slaves and at artisanal trades that earned money from the Union army. It had three churches, modest wood residences, and stores and businesses operated by African Americans. A government of military officers and a freely elected council established schools and sanitation codes, punished drunkenness and crime, enforced property rights, settled disputes, and collected taxes. Teachers came from the North's American Missionary Association, and for some four and a half hours a day children between six and fifteen had to attend school. In the antebellum South, planters sent their children to private academies and Northern colleges; they saw no need to subsidize public schooling for the yeomen farmers, and it was a crime for slaves to read, so illiteracy was high. African American Mitchelville was the first site of compulsory education in all of South Carolina.

But the town was short lived. The Union pay that had been the backbone of the economy left with the army in 1868, and although the town continued, the island's freedmen scattered, making a living by fishing and subsistence farming, some renting lands from the government and working in collectives. There were enough oysters in the island beds for whoever wanted them, and locally grown crops could be taken by boat to the Savannah markets. Sometimes the freedmen lived in the old plantation houses, usually two-story wooden structures built on stilts, with a wide piazza across the front. But Union forces had dismantled most of them for lumber, and storms and erosion washed many others away. Since most of the English-speaking whites had left, the freedmen who remained spoke an African-inspired dialect known as Gullah, their language and culture remaining intact because of their isolation from both whites and the mainland.

But the blacks never gained legal control of the land. By 1866 the U.S. government had acquired most of the island's plantations for nonpayment of taxes, and the Second Freedman's Bureau Act of that year required that unneeded lands be sold to heads of families. But for the most part these sales never happened. Assuming the presidency upon Lincoln's assassination a month after the war was won, Andrew Johnson gave away the opportunity to impose conditions on the South that would have made the victory over slavery economically meaningful. There was no general confiscation of Southern property and no land reform;

Johnson, a Tennessean, allowed planters to regain their land after paying their taxes and taking an "iron-clad oath" to support the Union. By also letting Confederates be seated in Congress simply upon taking the oath, Johnson nullified the freedom-based ideological nature of the victory that Lincoln had carefully worked to construct. It is for these reasons, along with his refusal to work with the Republican Congress representing the government that won the war, that Johnson was the only American president to be impeached; he escaped conviction by only one vote.

As Hilton Head acreage was restored to its former owners, some African Americans had to give back land they had already bought, although some planter families, like the Draytons, sold parcels to freedmen. A black speculator bought up the 165 or so acres on which Mitchelville was built, and later he and his family also sold lots to island blacks. Indeed, most of the freed people on Hilton Head who owned their land bought it. The legendary gift of forty acres and a mule was only the dream of a handful of radical Congressional Republicans; the Southern Homestead Act, the moderate compromise bill that actually became law, allowed both blacks *and* whites to settle on public lands in the frontier South, but the bill only served some twenty-seven thousand people, and there were four million emancipated slaves at the end of the Civil War.

According to most sources, between 1870 and 1930, Hilton Head's black population dwindled, although it is unlikely that census takers combed the island very thoroughly. In 1900, only about thirty-five hundred of the island's twenty-three thousand or so acres belonged to the people who called themselves native islanders, most of it held in five- to ten-acre parcels. By 1930, a wealthy New Yorker named Roy Rainey had already been buying up much of the island for hunting. And along about the 1950s a succession of developers and land speculators systematically acquired some 75 percent of the island and felled many of its pine trees at a profit. They were, however, careful about which trees they cut down, knowing full well that the island was "ripe for development."

Perhaps because the built environment is so new, the whole concept of the past seems remote and disconnected on Hilton Head. The only indication of Mitchelville is a historic marker by the roadside; only one former plantation house still stands; the island's museum is more of a cultural welcoming center than a repository of the past. And yet South Carolina has long tried to play on its history to lure tourists, using ads and brochures promoting the state's "hospitality" and "graciousness." The mythical lore of the Old South certainly played a part in developers' wholesale embrace of the word *plantation*, its connotation of wealth and luxurious living clearly central to their marketing strategies. But the word's association with slavery, remarkably, appears to go relatively unnoticed on the island. Of course, this phenomenon of forgetfulness about the Old South was also evident nationally in a recent issue of Civil War postage stamps that featured Robert E. Lee and Stonewall Jackson alongside Lincoln and Frederick Douglass, as if all were equally patriotic, as if they had no real differences between them. But they did. After 1830, the region that became the Confederacy was no embodiment of American ideals. Authoritarian and, for blacks, totalitarian, it proscribed education and restricted the press and mails. The culture of its antebellum elite was derivative, imitating the British aristocracy in its social mores and the ancient Greeks and Romans in its architecture, and produced virtually no artists whose work has lasted except that of the mad and troubled Edgar Allan Poe. Its religions embracing fervor rather than reason, the region isolated itself intellectually. The South's clear subjugation of the individual to the slave system took place in an era in which Russian serfdom and most of New World slavery—in the North, in most of the Caribbean, and in parts of South America—fell without violence in response to evolving post-Enlightenment views of Christianity, the self, and individual responsibility most famously expressed in the works of Ralph Waldo Emerson and Henry David Thoreau.

Johnson's failure to hold the South materially responsible for the costly, gruesome, and exhausting national war provided, it seemed to me, a key mechanism that enabled the South to live in a state of social irresponsibility and denial for such a long time. Until just recently, Southerners have been able to deflect discussion about the Confederacy from the issue of slavery to one of regionalist culture, claiming that the Confederate flag is about heritage rather than hate; but even viewed in the most charitable light, the desire to hang Confederate flags for reasons of heritage suggests a need to view the Civil War as somehow not connected to their region's economic mainstay, the enslavement of human beings. Indeed, even 140 years later, there is a sense in which suggesting that the Civil War was actually *about* something fundamental is a subject so taboo that it's difficult to discuss publicly in many places in the South.

49

This could not have been more apparent in the new television documentary history of Hilton Head that aired in town council chambers on my first night there. The heavy turnout, consisting largely of aging white Hilton Headers and a handful of African Americans, suggested that my Sea Pines guide was not the only one hungry for history. Funded in part by a grant from the town's tax on hotel rooms, the film was made up of four half-hour segments. The first examined a series of Paleo-Indian remains, and then presented the European comers without reference to their mission; it was easy to assume they were explorers. In the antebellum segment, slavery was mentioned only once and was in no way depicted as the foundation of the island's economy; for coverage of the Civil War, the film described the battle of Port Royal. A third section, focusing on the Gullah people and their traditions, featured people speaking the lilting West Indian–sounding dialect and demonstrating crafts such as weaving and net making; the final segment reveled in the developer vision that has shaped the island over the past forty years. Overall, the movie presented the island's past in bland and undisturbing terms. That *there was no mention of the causes of the Civil War*, as if the conflict that ended slavery had no relation to the American identity or human progress, struck me as both odd and terrifying.

Like a number of histories in the museum's gift shop, which euphemistically referred to "the war for Southern independence," the movie repeatedly used the term *contraband*, a word coined on the Union side to refer to African Americans fleeing to Union forces during the war. Its overuse seemed a sly effort to suggest that Northerners had also considered the slaves things, and were therefore no more morally superior in regard to blacks than white Southerners themselves. Northerners *were* decidedly racist, but there is a great deal of difference between racism, however gross, and the system of chattel slavery the Confederacy sought to defend. Besides, the term was hardly applied in malice. The Fugitive Slave Law was still in effect during the war, and some Union commanders were allowing slave masters to reclaim refugees who had taken cover with Union forces. To prevent this, the antislavery general Benjamin Butler took to calling the refugee bondsmen "contraband of war" on the grounds that they could be used by their owners to strengthen Confederate fortifications. The expression's practical effect, two years before formal emancipation, was freedom for enslaved persons.

The Harvard historian of slavery Orlando Patterson has described the slave system of the American South as "the last and most perfectly articulated slave culture since the fall of the Roman Empire." Some New World slave systems allowed slaves to become free by performing heroic acts, through marriage, and by several other means; in the American South, however, laws made it very difficult for the enslaved to become free, and the numbers of those who did so was much lower than in other systems. But unlike the Germans, who after World War II were subject to a denazification program that was in essence a moral reeducation, the American South was never, as a matter of policy, made to understand or repudiate the moral hideousness of slavery. If the civil rights era brought some repentance of segregation, that custom's deeper roots, in slavery, were left largely undisturbed.

The filmmakers, who hoped to start other film

projects on the island, had apparently believed that only by skirting the issue of slavery entirely could they reach a broad audience. And to judge from the favorable remarks of people leaving the showing, they had succeeded. As I filed out with them I thought how comfortable it must be to live in houses and communities composed of the clean, rational surfaces of late-twentieth-century American upper-middle-class life; to imagine a painless and inoffensive past; never to see even for an instant the LRTA riders as the direct descendants of American slaves: as if history were a box out of which isolated parts could be taken up and enjoyed each on its own, with no relation to a whole and no connecting narrative at all.

In speaking of the cultures of the various Hilton Head plantations, one developer has described "a set of tribes, the Sea Pines tribe, the Port Royal tribe," and indeed the plantations do have distinct personalities. Sea Pines, known for its large forest preserve and the island's only ostensible town at Harbour Town, seems, with its three-dollar day pass for the public, the most accessible and cosmopolitan. Although luxuriantly large and green, Hilton Head Plantation feels mostly like a number of amply spaced subdivisions grouped around a golf course. Wexford Plantation prides itself on being the wealthiest and most deluxe. Featuring a sort of English manor theme with old stone walking bridges, Wexford is secure even from the sea, with a system of locks for those entering the waterways within its boundaries. It has million-dollar homes with private yacht slips, and the street signs, a video advertising the plantation informs, are etched in twenty-four-karat gold. That's right. *The street signs are etched in twenty-four-karat gold.*

Hilton Head is a place where a conservative, inwardly turned, and socially unprogressive ethos has flourished. Numerous former officials of the notoriously secret CIA and State Department retire there, but more telling is that although the island's developments have been marketed nationally, they have tended to attract conservative Republicans. For a long time there was no Democratic Party on Hilton Head, the county chapter in Beaufort having simply written the island off as a Republican stronghold. A former academic who helped form Hilton Head's first Democratic club in the late 1980s was initially surprised by all the racism and stereotyping among the predominantly white plantation populace. "There were remarks about Japs and blacks and the most hideous condescension toward Democrats," she recalled of her first years on the island. The domination of conservative ideology has been so intense, according to insiders, that people with more liberal views either endure regular ribbings on the golf course or keep them hidden.

But in the late 1970s and early 1980s, change came in a guise that was deeply threatening to property owners who had made huge investments to seclude themselves in a land of beauty. With money flowing from deregulated savings and loans, developers and venture capitalists with little commitment to the island began building hotels and vacation villas and time-share condos, and soon the population increased dramatically. Malls and shopping centers sprang up and, needing an ever-larger customer base, began to

try and attract people from the mainland to shop on
Hilton Head. Traffic woes increased; noise and litter
and crowding came too, and many residents fanta-
sized about blowing up the bridge to keep the new
paradise seekers out. The last straw came with the sud-
den appearance of prefabricated vacation villas (immediately dubbed "stack-a-shacks") on Route 278,
architectural mediocrities that seemed to herald the
arrival of the lower classes and the equally dreaded
strip commercial. But the county government up
in Beaufort was rubber-stamping those Hilton Head
building permits because the new buildings meant
tax revenues in a decade when public funds had been
slashed, and the county government was the only
government there was.

After the failure of various antidevelopment
schemes, plantation dwellers realized that only municipal incorporation and a public government could
pass legislation that would stop the overbuilding. A
municipality could enforce zoning, which the authors
of a recent study of race and housing have called "the
chief instrument by which suburbs have held themselves apart from the poor." But since the vast majority of Hilton Head property owners felt that less
government was best, the proposed new local government would have to be made to seem minimalist.
*Town* was clearly a less threatening term than *city*, and
then the phrase *limited services government* was tossed
into the debate. Legally, there is no such thing. The
incorporation articles for the Town of Hilton Head
Island say nothing about such a concept, and almost
everyone I spoke to conceded, when pressed, that
it was basically just a sales pitch. Yet both the town-
funded documentary and an urban designer in Town

Hall used the term freely, and I heard it often enough
to understand that it is firmly lodged in the Hilton
Head imagination and hangs over the island's politics
like a shroud.

To many native islanders, the plantation development
of the 1960s and 1970s seemed like a juggernaut.
Blacks had made up 90 percent of the population in
the 1950s, but by 1990 they represented only 8 percent. As developers marketed Hilton Head nationally,
more and more whites arrived who knew nothing
about their Gullah culture and did not care to learn.
Some, like those from wealthy Northern suburbs who
knew few blacks at work or in their neighborhoods,
brought with them negative stereotypes of urban
blacks that had nothing to do with the native islanders. Moreover, the term *plantation* reminded
African Americans of slavery, and many of them felt
that all those manned gates were meant to keep them
out of white territory.

Rightly fearful that white property owners would
monopolize the proposed government simply by de-
mographics, most island blacks opposed incorporation. The idea of a limited services government was
particularly anathema since it suggested higher property taxes without the improvements in water and
sewer service, police protection, housing, and recreation that a regular municipality would offer. But
NAACP legal challenges to incorporation failed.
Most blacks voted against it, and a number apparently
declined to vote. "Native islanders did not participate in the incorporation because that was a way of
protesting," the town's black councilman told me,
confirming the view voiced by another black leader.

"The thought was that the whites would take notice of this and talk with us." This unstated belief in the social consciences of the plantation dwellers, however, was clearly misplaced.

Just as there are avenues into the past that can be completely avoided, parts of the island are nearly invisible to many plantation dwellers and vacationers, and they bear no resemblance to the rest of neatly groomed and modern Hilton Head. Here are little dirt lanes hosting trailers and one-story modular or red-brick houses with propane tanks outside. Sometimes these small communities, hidden by vegetation screens and trees, adjoin golf courses around which expensive homes have been built. Sometimes they abut brand-new developments from which they are separated only by tall stockade fences. To see the real estate maxim of "location, location, location" being so blatantly disregarded is to understand how valuable all land is on Hilton Head, and to get a sense of the pressure to sell under which people who own undeveloped land must live.

This is Ward One, and it is home to many of the descendants of the island's freedmen and to my Sea Pines guide, who commuted an hour each way for seven years but now lives on the island in a trailer. Housing prices are so high that mobile homes are all many young couples can afford, and there are precious few affordable rentals on the island. Ward One landowners pay property taxes just like other islanders, but the area has only the most limited access to services such as paved roads and town water and sewers. Black leaders complained about this even in 1974, nine years before incorporation; today, the same problems remain. The town has, however, named the

little unpaved streets, and they are marked with permanent, uniform signs. "Isn't that nice," the councilman remarked drily.

When the town was incorporated, the developers'
CID plans for Hilton Head's plantations, for the most
part already built and obviously including paved roads
and water and sewer service, were accepted in toto as
the town-approved plans for those areas. Ward One,
however, had never been the domain of a private developer, and in thirteen years the town still has not
planned it. The white plantation dwellers who dominate the political system have never seen delivering
basic services as part of the price of being involved in a
municipality. Moreover, the town implemented its development controls when the plantations were completed but when blacks were only just beginning to
gain enough from the island's prosperity to begin development themselves. In 1991, however, native islanders made their discontent clear to thirty million
American viewers on the television program *60
Minutes*.

Indeed, national attention to the gross disparities
has been the only significant impetus to reform. In
late 1994, the black councilman, frustrated at not being able to pass a single piece of legislation for his
ward in two years, began calling the media. CNN, the
*Atlanta Constitution*, and the *New York Times* all ran
major stories about the situation on Hilton Head, and
the United States Justice Department confirmed the
councilman's charges that representation on the island had not been equitable. All this embarrassed or
in some way nudged the town council into looking at
the problem, and in response to the town's applica-
tion, the American Institute of Architects sent a

Regional Urban Design Assistance Team (RUDAT)
down to study the development possibilities for Ward
One.

The situation did not warrant their usual type of report, however. "This RUDAT is not a study of design or
planning but of a chronic failure of a town to meet
its obligations," the authors of the team's report con-
cluded bluntly:

> There is a serious and apparently permanent inequity
> in the way the town has used its powers to accomplish
> what the residents of the plantations clearly want for
> this island. They wish to impose stringent development
> controls and protracted growth limitations on the own-
> ers of property in Ward One and the native residents of
> this island. They have used growth control ordinances
> and traffic impact fees, the refusal to extend basic ser-
> vices, and the recurrent refrain that the Town is a 'lim-
> ited services government' to avoid the Town's basic
> duties to the residents and property owners of Ward
> One. . . . The first residents of the island became the last
> to benefit from this development, and the Town has
> now told them essentially that they must sacrifice their
> right to services and development for the greater good
> of limiting growth on the island.

The language of the report was so unambiguous
that at its presentation in Town Hall supporters gave it
a standing ovation. It was, as one town planner told
me, "a kind of a wake-up call."

"Limited services government was politically unrealis-
tic," a Princeton expert on development has said of
Hilton Head. But it was more than that. It was a lie
perpetrated to get a constituency that had turned its
back on public government to erect one, while assur-
ing them that they would not have to take responsibil-

ity for other people. Perhaps, as the councilman suggested, buyers saw themselves as a kind of royalty who deserved to live a life apart in splendor. Certainly, developers and real estate companies encouraged these fantasies, feeding buyers the illusion of a life completely removed from social problems. And perhaps residents bought the lie because they were living under private CID governments fostering a nonparticipatory culture in which owning property suggests autonomy and individualism rather than political obligations. Living in modernized environments that never suggest a past that might allow them to feel connected to other centuries or to the great experiment of our nation, isolated behind their security gates, plantation dwellers thought, most audaciously, that they could extend their myopic embrace of class separatism to a legally constituted American government.

Development continues to move forward in the Coastal Empire, as the area between Charleston and Savannah is called. On the mainland across from the island, Del Webb is building a retirement community called Sun City Hilton Head that will bring a projected sixteen thousand CID residents to the area, and farther west near I-95 Disney and the Automobile Club of America are planning a $38 million "thematic travel center" for tourists, a commercial village on an American Main Street theme that, as a project architect declares, "really revives a sense of history." But it is frightening to think that this kind of history is the only one we will need. Through its mortgage programs, our national government has curtailed the power of its local affiliates and unwittingly sacrificed local democratic rule to the forces of capital. Indeed,

Americans tend to profoundly confuse democracy and
capitalism, but the struggle to maintain democracy in
the face of a moneyed elite has always been a part of
our history. "This is essentially a people's contest,"
Lincoln declared to Congress in 1861. "It is a struggle
for maintaining in the world, that form and substance
of government whose leading object is to elevate the
condition of men—to lift artificial weights from all
shoulders." And it is still for us today "to be here dedicated to the great task remaining before us," to ensure
"that government of the people, by the people, for the
people, shall not perish from the earth."

## Entertainment Capitals

From Bill Cody's Wild West shows to the Hollywood musi-
cals of the Depression years, Americans have long loved to
be entertained; today the show-biz gossip shows follow right
after the evening news, and the star syndrome has prevailed
in fields from academia to publishing. But mega-scale
locales devoted exclusively to entertainment were new.
Descendants of Coney Island and Disneyland, these were
separate worlds to which Americans removed themselves
from the stress and complication of everyday life for days at
a time and solely for enjoyment. The area around Orlando,
the number-one vacation destination in the nation, nicknamed Hollywood East, hosted the greatest number of such
worlds. In the last three decades, Sea World, Flea World,
Disney World, Universal Studios, Disney/MGM, Starbase
Omega, and Xanadu had been plopped down as if from
space onto the once-nowhere open territory of Central
Florida.

    Sometimes what passed for entertainment seemed trou-
bling and strange: In 1992 the producers of a Mel Gibson
police-and-mayhem blockbuster had paid the City of
Orlando $50,000 to film for its opening scene the spectacu-
lar demolition of the old-fashioned Orlando city hall, become too small for a boomtown; waiting for the elevator to
the parking garage at Trump Plaza in Atlantic City, I'd
watched a video monitor play a film in which a stately
boardwalk hotel, from the Victorian days when the town
had been an oasis of air and light a train ride away from the
hot red brick of Philadelphia, was dynamited again and
again to make way for a casino. When I thought about the

61

endless car chases and shoot-outs that were standard fare in the movies, I wondered at how enamored of destruction we'd become.

But my subject was less the content of entertainment than the fact that it was an industry which occupied an increasing amount of the landscape and the economy. Between 1980 and 1987, amusement and recreation revenues as a portion of the Gross National Product nearly doubled, helped along by places like Las Vegas or Atlantic City or Deadwood or Laughlin, which were devoted almost entirely to gambling. Theme parks had reached new levels of sophistication and size and variety. There were the movie and nature worlds in Florida, the shopping and variety worlds of places like Dollywood, the righteous worlds of the Christian parks. So when I began to hear about a new country music capital in the Ozarks that was attracting millions of people a year and huge corporate investment sums, it seemed a likely place to investigate.

# Hub of the Hinterlands

Driving east from the grand Olmsted parks and substantial brick residences of faded Kansas City, the flat,
immobile landscapes along the interstate speak of
nothing so much as the long-gone vitality of the
American heartland. These were counties once connected to the big Midwest cities by railroads, counties
that delivered their livestock to the great packing-
houses in Kansas City or bought McCormick reapers
to harvest the grain they shipped to Chicago. As the
twentieth century began, their towns' Main Streets
were filled with leather goods and hardware and feed
stores and all the incredible and various merchandise
the railroads could bring. At century's end, however,
they are dried up, sun bleached, and cluttered with
abandoned stores, and on their outskirts Wal-Marts,
gas stations, and fast-food restaurants play to the no-
frills needs of those remaining. Heading south into
the Ozarks from this is a green relief. Down toward the
Arkansas border, the small towns appearing at odd
junctures along the lush and curving roads were never
really connected to the big markets. St. Louis, a river
city anyway, declined with the rise of Chicago, and the
Missouri Pacific was not completed until 1907. Plenty
of these dot-on-the-map Ozark towns have almost no
commerce at all, the only signs of culture the Church
of Christ or Baptist churches with their Wednesday
night prayer meetings and weekly services and Sunday
schools and suppers. Family, community, God—and
little else. And yet between these two time-stopped

landscapes little Branson, Missouri became a boomtown in the eighties and nineties, a country music
headquarters that draws five million tourists a year
and now lures even the corporate players, a clean-cut,
wager-free Christian entertainment mecca with a
miracle neon mile to light up the dark Missouri night.

I had flown into Kansas City and driven a rental
car for four hours, a routine I also could have followed
from Tulsa or St. Louis, because flying directly into
Branson would have increased my airfare by 150
percent. But the highway is the way most people
come, since the town is the nation's number one vacation destination by car behind Orlando. In the late
August afternoon heat I exited the freeway, passed
some road construction, and saw the sign for my
Rodeway or Ramada or Days Inn that could have been
anywhere, a brand-new brick block in the middle of
a paved parking lot, its minuscule pool alive with
shrieking children.

What about those wooded Ozark hills they'd
crowed about? But checking in brought only the un-
welcome news that the room was now twenty dollars
more than when I'd made the reservation. The final
blow, however, came when I unlocked the door to the
chamber itself. It was so new it smelled distinctly of
formaldehyde, and it overlooked a lot where an asphalt paving machine still sat over its steaming and
darkly completed work.

I do not remember the exact way in which I expressed my displeasure. I feel certain that I used the
word *carcinogen*, however, and the desk clerk, a fortyish white man, looked genuinely shocked and for a
moment blank, as if struggling to recall something
important, probably his customer service training.

But no, he really could not call around to other places when he had so many vacancies, and no, he really could not give me the lower price because he was already quoting me a significant discount off the rack rate.

"But I can put you in a room on the fourth floor, ma'am," he offered in an accent softly Southern, as if intuitively sensing that I did not care to drive even one mile farther. "You'll see the treetops from your room, and hardly anyone uses that pool until the afternoon. You can have it all to yourself in the morning. We have a steamroom, too," he added, "and complimentary coffee and Dunkin' Donuts every morning. Would you like to look at the fourth floor, ma'am? I can give you a choice of several rooms. They've been in service longer than the one you looked at, and maybe you'll like the smell better."

What could I say?

The fourth-floor room did not smell and indeed looked onto a verdant view, and later I asked the clerk where I could get dinner. Now that he had all the information he needed, he was calm and relaxed. "Actually," he leaned over the counter confidentially, "there's a place right next door that serves some of the best barbecue in the mountains."

So I walked over to a little trailer with a window cut out of the side, and the barbecue, which I had with a Coke at a shaded plastic table on the asphalt, was indeed excellent. The barbecue man had been to New York, it turned out. There, finding himself completely overwhelmed by all the activity, he had asked a nearby policeman for assistance. "Just move it along, buddy," the cop had barked, and now, recounting the tale, he was still a little hurt, a little offended, and more than

65

a little bewildered. Friendliness, I realized, was simply taken for granted in Branson.

Back at the hotel, the clerk gave me the phone number of a local radio host he thought I should speak to. And that was the way a lot of Branson was. I ran into a couple of fascistic ticket takers, to be sure, but most of the people there were just really, really nice.

Branson acquired some minor fame in 1907, when its hills provided the setting for Harold Bell Wright's popular novel *The Shepherd of the Hills*. But it only began to make a reliable living in 1913, when the White River on which it was located was dammed to the east. Branson's part of the river was suddenly turned into Lake Taneycomo—for Taney County, Missouri—and for some forty years Branson lured swimmers, boaters, and recreational fishermen. The little Main Street walking town had a café and a chain drug store and a five-and-ten and three or four other blocks of stores, many of them fronting on shaded sidewalks; it had a movie house called the Hillbilly Theater and the Hollywood Hills Hotel to serve vacationers. But in the late 1950s, the Army Corps of Engineers built another dam, this time to the west, and the resulting Table Rock Lake, an enormous body of water that could accommodate just about every water sport, for some reason left Lake Taneycomo so cold that only the fish would swim in it. This set the businesspeople and hucksters in town to brainstorming. Caves had figured in *The Shepherd of the Hills* and Mark Twain had long ago made Missouri caving an American legend, so when a spectacular and intricate underground cave

nine miles from Branson ran out of its eminently sell-
able stores of bat guano, an enterprising Chicago couple took a ninety-nine-year lease on it. Charging for
cave tours became so profitable that the couple built
a railroad into the cave and an ice cream parlor, stage-
coach ride, and craft shops in a little mountain village
called Silver Dollar City. Another family had come up
with the idea of staging *The Shepherd* in an outdoor
theater on the land where the characters inspiring the
book had lived; it too prospered, and its owners added
an amusement park. In 1960, five brothers named
Mabe, who enjoyed dressing up as hillbillies and calling themselves the Baldknobbers after an old Ozark
vigilante moonshine gang, began performing a country music show on the Branson lakefront. When a
family named Presley—no relation to Elvis—also
staged a successful country music show, the rest became, as they say, history.

In the 1960s and 1970s, country musicians of all
kinds began moving in bit by bit, and Branson began
spreading out from the old waterfront and along
Highway 76 in the now-familiar commercial-strip pattern. But it wasn't until the 1980s that the downtown
became a bit of nostalgia and no longer where it was
at. In those years, the Hee-Haw and the Starlite and
the Wilkinson Brothers' theaters were built; Presley's
Mountain Music Jubilee expanded to 2,000 seats; and
the Swiss Villa, Echo Hollow, and Ozark Mountain am-
phitheaters, seating some 19,500 people, also went up.
The Roy Clark Celebrity Theatre was the first to be
connected to a widely known entertainer, and soon
Box Car Willie moved in. As the 1990s began, Willie
Nelson, Glen Campbell, Kenny Rogers, Johnny Cash,

Merle Haggard, and the Gatlin Brothers all began appearing in Branson, and many theaters extended the
season for Christmas. "Old country music stars never
die," a Nashville observer has declared. "They just
move to Branson," and soon mainstream musicians
joined them. Bobby Vinton, Andy Williams, and
Tony Orlando have recently built theaters, and John
Davidson, who used to rent his space at some thirty
thousand dollars a month, has also performed ener-
getically and profitably in town. Even the Lawrence
Welk organization has built a resort in Branson, and
magic shows, puppet shows, and gospel shows can be
found in staggering array. The town claims more theater seats than Broadway and more regularly sched-
uled performances than anywhere else in the nation.

The freewheeling 1980s produced splendid state-of-
the-art theaters in Branson. The most ambitious of
these, like the Grand Palace or the Five Star, have
imposing outdoor façades with cupolas or balconies
or the huge white columns of plantations; the
Shenandoah sits high atop a hill like a Southern
Baptist church overseeing the land below. The lobbies
of these theaters are sometimes marvelously large.
Light-filled descendants of early-twentieth-century
movie theaters such as Loew's Grand or RKO Proctors,
they hark back to a time when going out to a show
was an innocent and safe activity for couples, and if
beneath their soaring ceilings their patrons are tread-
ing the plush carpets of deluxe hotels or the marble
flooring of the better shopping malls, they are usually
snacking on popcorn and Coke.

Indeed, the people who come to see shows in
Branson are totally unpretentious, as well as solidly

white, Christian, and middle and working class. Many
are retirees who arrive on the more than fourteen
thousand motor coaches pulling into Branson each
year from as far away as Canada and the East Coast
and Washington State. In the summer, children come
with their parents to enjoy the bumper cars, mini golf,
bungee jumping, water slides, amusement arcades,
and funnel cake parlors that line Highway 76 between
the theaters, motels, and all-you-can-eat buffet restaurants. But whatever their ages, there is nothing in
Branson to frighten them. There are no prostitutes,
gambling, drugs, or rowdy drinking. Even the sex
jokes told at shows are about married life or adolescent attempts to neck in the backseats of cars. And
most of "the stars" try to show how they are like the
audiences, either through their families or their religion. Just as the author of *The Shepherd of the Hills* has
been called "the most ridiculed writer of his generation," so can few serious musicians bring themselves
to speak of a "creative level" in Branson. More than
anything Branson reveals the huge numbers of
Americans between the coasts who live in a world
that is deeply provincial and culturally starved.

*The Shepherd of the Hills*, said to be the most attended
outdoor drama in America, has been seen by more
than one million people during its thirty-six-year run
in Branson, and the author of the original novel,
Harold Bell Wright, was once a household name. By
1918, his seven novels had enjoyed combined sales of
more than seven million copies, and this average of
a million copies a book was something of a world's
record. Newspaper lore has it that for some twenty

years Wright's books outsold all others except the Bible.

Although of painterly and literary bent, Wright was a country preacher for ten years, embracing nonsectarian Christianity mostly because it offered a plan for right living. When he left the pulpit to write full time, he considered his writing a "ministry of print" through which he could reach audiences far larger than congregations. His novels, not surprisingly, are a bit like morality plays, lively and readable, but predictable and stagy. These qualities deterred neither his millions of fans nor Hollywood, however, which made four versions of *The Shepherd*, one starring John Wayne.

Hardly accidentally, Wright's publisher, Book Supply Company of Chicago, did not market his books through the traditional literary markets in urban centers. Instead, they advertised in religious journals like the Methodist *Zion Herald*, regional newspapers like the *St. Louis Globe-Democrat*, and widely popular magazines such as the *Saturday Evening Post*, hoping to reach people in small towns and distant farms and ranches who didn't have much exposure to the book market. When a Wright novel came out, orders from such places far surpassed those from urban retailers, and the books were made available through rural drug, general, and grocery stores.

These small towns and villages are the same places from which Branson's tourists largely come, from Franklin, Idaho, or Fred, Kansas, or Cummings, Nebraska, places that are isolated and distant from mainstream cultural outlets. And just as in *The Shepherd* the wise man has left the city for the mountains, part of Branson's attraction for its audience is that, although often host to 50,000 people a day in the high season, its year-round population is only 3,700, so that it can fairly be described as a small town. For if the reasons have changed from swindles, white slavery, and syphilis in the past one hundred years to random violence, drug abuse, and AIDS, fear of cities is still a potent theme in rural America.

Branson never found itself on either the westward migration routes of blacks after the Civil War or their northern urban migration in the twentieth century, and unlike people from urban and suburban places, people in Branson seem to have had only limited contact with diversity. Branson's year-round population, according to the 1990 census, contains only two black people, ten Native Americans, and twenty-five Asians. Entertainers from other countries, like the Japanese violinist Shoji Tabuchi or the Russian comedian Yakov "What a Country" Smirnoff, know they are anomalies. "A lot of people are surprised that I speak English," Shoji says, confronting the Asian stereotype head-on before launching into a violin rendition of "Them Old Cotton Fields Back Home," and Yakov's phone number is 1-800-4NO-KGB just in case anyone's worried. Both entertainers play on their love of America to connect with an audience that has had little contact with foreigners.

Like those in the little Ozark towns, Branson's visitors seem somewhat innocent of the marketplace. Before the Grand Palace Shopping Mall opened in Branson in 1994, people in the area had to drive fifty miles to Springfield to go to a bookstore, and it is likely that things are not much better in towns on the Great Plains or Texas. "It's been incredibly difficult to find furniture for my house," a Branson musician told me, suggesting too that the tourist predilection for clothes found at Wal-Marts or Kmarts meant that the markets had never really reached to where they lived. With limited exposure to big business, the people in this solidly Republican town where George Bush kicked off his 1992 campaign seemed to see the GOP not as a party of the rich but as a force bringing jobs and manufactured items and culture.

Yet "the environment is important to everybody," said the city administrator of Branson. "Entertainment is big but underlying it are the scenic hills and lakes." The City levies heavy fines for trees removed without a permit; and when I was in town, Kenny Rogers was pushing an eco-friendly home development and launched the *Branson Belle*, a showboat on which visitors can enjoy dinner, a show, and a three-hour cruise on Table Rock Lake. Eighty crates of biodegradable bananas lubricated the launching rails while the huge ship was pushed into the water by bulldozers; the vessel is powered by Soy Diesel, a biodegradable fuel made from soybeans. "It provides cleaner emissions . . . and it's a boon to American soybean farmers as well," a spokesman for the Missouri Soybean Merchandising Council declared.

"People come to Branson in groups," one writer has observed. "Family groups. Community groups. Retirement groups. Church groups," and it was clear to me that they are exactly those to whom the "family values" rhetoric, so hollow-sounding to many on the coasts, is pitched. They did not seem alienated, and apparently had different coping mechanisms for the troubles of life. Anita Byrant wore the army flak jacket of a boy killed in Vietnam over an evening gown to sing armed forces songs, and among the audience were couples who must have lost children in the wars, living in tiny towns where there was little to take their minds off heartbreak, and they wept as Bryant spoke of their pain. Later she sang "The Battle Hymn of the Republic," and a huge flag dropped down behind her. Her show was disturbing because it seemed more an intensely driven attempt to validate her beliefs than an aesthetically coherent entertainment. Her life had been shattered, I read in a gift shop autobiography, by her divorce and the impact her antigay views had had on her career. Johnny Cash, the proverbial man in black whose drug problems have been legendary, also sang songs of faith, and his band, I learned at a party, is not allowed to drink even beer. More than Prozac or therapy or substances, in Branson patriotism and religious fervor were widely accepted and used as the treatment of choice for despair.

"Where you heading?" the desk clerk always asked casually whenever I walked through the lobby toward the front door, and as soon as they got in their cars and had the seat belts on, Branson natives would ask what time it was. If shows were about to go on or were just getting out, traffic along Highway 76 could be a nightmare, and it was essential to plan an alternate route to avoid losing an hour getting from one end of town to the other. The traffic woes underscored the lack of planning that had accompanied most of the development, but as of 1994 no feasible mass transit solution could be devised, since everything was located along 76. Although residents had found a way to cope by using the back roads, routes under construction, theater parking lots, and other shortcuts, the problems with traffic were a reminder of how built up Branson was becoming, how much like a city it was getting to be. It was a boomtown with interstates being built around it, a place attracting GM and Radisson and the $10 billion Carlton Hospitality Group. Once I was waiting at a red light when the people in the car beside me motioned for me to roll down my window. "Grand-a Palace" they kept repeating, having no flair for sentences, and as I answered them in Spanish I realized that the rest of America would be coming to Branson after all.

A few minutes before the show, the lobby of the purple-and-pink Shoji Tabuchi Theater was packed. I had been told that the ladies' room was part of the Shoji experience, so I maneuvered myself to stand in line for it. Pressed among hundreds of women, I became aware that my fellow theatergoing ladies had none of the respect for personal boundaries long residence in New York had instilled in me. I felt a hand on my forearm—the woman behind me. Glancing back, I saw that she looked about sixty and perfectly healthy, her hair set in a beauty parlor wave. I gathered, from her grasp, that she was seeking some kind of security and hoped to be guided by a younger person through the massive throng, and then I was a little astonished. She continued to hold on as if certain she would be safe with me, and I found, in this lack of caution, a profound trust and innocence that was unusual and refreshing. I led her through the crowd.

The ladies' room was worth the wait, and the wash area was truly outstanding. Brightened by afternoon sunlight that filtered through a haze of lace curtains, it had fluted glass sconces and an abundance of silk ivy and lilacs; the deep green pressed-tin ceiling gave it a turn-of-the-century flourish. Above the gold-fauceted sinks hung gilt-framed mirrors, and in the middle of the carpeted room a glass cart held Eternity, Escape, L'Air du Temps, and various perfumed hand lotions, dispensed by a blond, longhaired, thirtysomething Southern belle in décolleté who clearly reveled in her position. I washed my face, combed my hair, put on powder, lipstick, and some Shalimar, and headed out for the show feeling pleasantly refreshed.

The ushers in the huge new theater, in white gloves and black uniforms with gold epaulets and trim, were helping a number of theatergoers with walkers to their seats. Then the *Star Wars* music came on full-volume and computer-generated graphics moved endlessly on the stage curtain until we were finally off. Girls in tight dresses danced with guys in bright blazers to a rock tune called "We're So Excited" that turned into a patriotic number where big-haired women in se-quined evening gowns called out the names of all fifty states. There was a harem number with teenage Christina Tobuchi coming down on a magic carpet; there was a genie in a bottle and some fog. And finally Shoji himself, looking like his hair had been cut with a bowl, emerged in sequined jacket. He was an energetic violinist, playing things like "Won't You Come Home, Bill Bailey," "When the Saints Come Marching In," and Dixieland jazz, and sometimes his instrument was outlined in neon on the dark stage, along with the boots and caps of dancers. Later, women in leotards with big cow heads came on, and in no time there were steel drums and it was "Yellow Bird." Some skinny Elvis impersonators appeared, and then a Mr. M.C. Hammerhead come out, handing the band turned-around baseball caps and rapping the story of

Jed Clampett. Later there were the polkas and bubbles of *The Lawrence Welk Show*. The whole thing was a nonstop lurch from one kind of popular music to another in no discernible order, and I only knew the finale was coming because of the obligatory gospel hymn and a choir-robed chorus that clapped its hands:

> *Oh, He's High*
> *And He's Mi-ight-y*
> *And He saved my soul for me . . .*

Soon, however, the show turned into another Vanna White number where women in red, white, and blue gowns talked of the Constitution signers and glorious freedom and sang "The Battle Hymn of the Republic." I was trying to muster every ounce of understanding that I could, but I still had to walk out before it was over, enraged almost to the point of nausea.

The show's condescension toward the audience was simply too much to bear. Careful to reinforce the narrow worlds the audience knew, the show's organizers had made sure there were no significant attempts to open new ones. "Make it loud, they're deaf," I could imagine them saying. "And give them plenty of flags and gospel 'cause they don't know anything else." Every time I saw a show like Tobuchi's I was struck by how forced upon Branson the patriotic and religious themes were, tried-and-true economic insurance policies, clumsily and artificially imposed. There were exceptions, of course: Tony Orlando staged a musical about a young man trying to make it in show business, and other entertainers with national reputations, like Andy Williams, also omitted the flag and religion entirely. But entertainers who did not physically embody traditional white male authority, like the black

country music singer Charlie Pride or Anita Bryant or
foreigners like Shoji or Smirnoff, seemed to feel oblig-
ated to play these cards. The overall effect was the
crude overkill of propaganda.

Outside Branson I drove across a bridge spanning
an Ozark lake as beautiful as any I had ever seen,
splendid and blue and calm with voluptuous trees
right up to its edge. With a growing population and
many other locations overdeveloped, it was inevitable
that this still beautiful part of America would be discovered. Producers and investors wanting a sure thing
were clamping a variation of the culture industries'
predictable formulas on Branson performances, and
because the town made money the corporations were
now attracted to it like vultures to a carcass. This sense
of enforced artificiality bothered me because Branson
itself was so sui generis. Neither city nor suburb nor
small town, it was a place whose popularity had
spread by word of mouth across the Bible Belt and farther west over the years. Its tourists just wanted to
have a good time and see professionally staged and
reasonably priced entertainment in one stress-free location; it supported the arts by enabling scores of professional musicians to earn stable, dependable livings.
It was not the product of huge economic forces like
Disney World but of people neither respected nor
much thought of by those on the coasts.

I headed back to Kansas City on the interstate. It
was clear that my explorations into the world created
by big business would be better directed elsewhere.

# Free-for-All

*During the Reagan "revolution" of the 1980s, great tax
breaks were given to businesses so that they could invest, expand their operations, create jobs, and thereby vindicate the
so-called trickle-down theory of economics. And before the
stock market tumbled in late 1987, a feeling of prosperity
and impressive growth reigned, especially in law, finance,
and real estate. But a perilous and unsavory growth also
took place and for a while went unrecognized, flourishing in
part because greed had somehow been transformed from a
vice into a creative, energizing, and even patriotic adjunct to
free enterprise. This malignant growth left many permanent
marks on the Sun Belt landscape from Florida to California,
where it spawned buildings for the simple reason that their
investors had fortunes to win and nothing at all to lose. The
funds they built with, of course, were insured by American
taxpayers under the Federal Savings and Loan Insurance
Corporation (FSLIC).*

*Set up to specialize in home mortgages and so different
from ordinary commercial banks, savings and loan (S&L)
associations first opened in this country in Pennsylvania in
1831. They were a natural in a land where so many people
dreamed of owning their homes, and for a long time they
kept the idea of home buying morally pure and elevated from
the crass competition of commercial capitalism. Earning the
nickname "thrifts," savings and loan associations carried
on a conservative, predictable business, paying modest interest on savings deposits that they then lent out to local
home buyers in long-term mortgages. Things went along
fine until the stock market crashed in 1929 and the Great*

*Depression hit. As the economy screeched wretchedly to a
halt and the building trades lost some 90 percent of their
contracts, about 1,700 thrifts went under, taking some two
hundred million depositor dollars with them.*

*The hapless Herbert Hoover tried to restore confidence
and help the housing industry by creating the Federal Home
Loan Bank Board and regulating the thrifts under its pur-
view. But Americans who'd lost their life savings in thrifts
wouldn't go near them until Franklin Roosevelt insured their
deposits under the FSLIC, funded by assessments on member thrifts. Roosevelt's plan worked for fifty years. And, still
required by law to invest only in residential mortgages, savings and loans again became identified with stability and
the success of the little guy. Through 30-year, fixed-rate
mortgages that helped the new middle class afford houses,
thrifts largely financed the great postwar migration to the
suburbs; they "provided the fuel for the home-building engine that for almost half a century acted as the fountainhead
of America's dynamic domestic economy," the authors of
a history of the savings and loan scandal recall. Indeed,
America's economic health came to be measured in housing
starts. Securely wrapped in their affable local-business garb,
thrifts remained quietly in their profitable niche until the
late 1970s, when they began rather quickly to wither and die.*

*The problem was inflation. Under Jimmy Carter, con-
sumer prices had risen about 10 percent each year, and in
1979, to combat this, the Federal Reserve Bank decided to let
interest rates float instead of keeping a lid on them. In no
time, money markets were paying up to 14 percent, and nobody wanted to invest in savings and loans, which could
still only pay some 5.5 percent. So thrifts began hemorrhag-
ing deposits. Their combined wealth dropped from $16.7
billion in 1972 to a net worth of minus $17.5 billion eight*

years later; 85 percent of them were losing money. Warning
that "confidence in the entire financial system could evapo-
rate," federal regulators predicted that if the problem were
left unchecked, every savings and loan would be wiped out
by 1986.

In other crises, regulators had simply added more regulations. But perhaps because inflation seemed a formidable
foe, or because the Reagan antigovernment message was beginning to get through, or perhaps because regulators didn't
know what else to do, deregulation became the cry, and
Congress answered with the Depository Institutions
Deregulation and Monetary Control Act in 1980. Unfortunately, this act, which phased out interest controls, also
raised the deposit amounts insured by the FSLIC from
$40,000 to $100,000, a colossal but as yet unrealized mis-
take. Thrifts could now offer competitive interest and began
accepting brokered deposits in blocks of up to $100,000,
known as "hot money" because it moved around daily in
search of higher returns. But the problem had hardly been
solved. The deposit side of the ledger had been straightened
out, but the money on loan to pay interest on those deposits
was still tied up in modestly paying long-term mortgages.
And as one chronicler put it, "You didn't need to be a genius
to understand that if you were borrowing money at 16 percent and lending it out at 8 percent, you wouldn't remain in
business for very long."

But what could the thrifts do? And rather than risk a
run on deposits and collapse, they resigned themselves to
paying higher interest and kept right on losing record
amounts of money. Industry lobbyists again yelled for help,
and Congress devised the Garn-St. Germain Depository
Institutions Act of 1982, which Ronald Reagan jauntily
signed into law in the Rose Garden. "All in all," the Great

Communicator exulted at the ceremony, "I think we've hit the jackpot."

"Bet the bank" was more like it. Garn-St. Germain was sweeping, heavy-handed legislation that shoved the highly regulated thrifts straight into the free market, to which they had never been exposed. Suddenly they could offer money market accounts and make up to 40 percent of their loans in commercial ventures, and regulators followed these with even more changes. Thrifts were now allowed to put up 100 percent financing and make loans anywhere; they could be owned not just by a group of stockholders but by simply one shareholder, hopefully a daring entrepreneurial wizard who would save the day. As a further incentive to take over these losing businesses, new owners could buy thrifts by putting up land or other noncash assets. To top it all off, Congress, trying to reassure a by-now suspicious public, also passed a resolution putting the full faith and credit of the American government behind the FSLIC.

Reagan and the Congress might just as well have held open the doors to the federal coffers and hollered, "Come and get it, boys!" The book titles alone—High Rollers, Inside Job, Other People's Money, Who Robbed America?—convey the gist of the sordid tale that followed. Almost as soon as these changes were made, greedy people of all kinds began to see that borrowing from a savings and loan was a no-risk venture. And they soon found varied and creative ways of borrowing the taxpayers' money and making their fortunes with it. New S&L owners could pay themselves huge bonuses, skim loans to overvalued properties, pocket loan points and originating fees, or finance their own dream projects. Pensions funds were deposited, money laundered; the Gambino, Genovese, Lucchese, and other crime families circled in. One man built a huge empire selling de-

*posits to looting S&L owners. Then too, many owners just
systematically looted their S&Ls and bought themselves
mansions and Rolls-Royces and leather-lined jets and
European junkets in five-star hotels and parties with live entertainment and paid-for women. Millions floated into
casino deals. Some thrifts used the money to influence legislators to keep the regulators at bay; Charles Keating, you
may recall, donated $1.4 million to the campaigns or causes
of Senators Alan Cranston, John Glenn, Donald Riegle,
John McCain, and Dennis DeConcini.*

*Reagan thought deregulation was one of his greatest tri-
umphs, so from 1982 to 1986, when the looting was really
a-go-go, nobody in his administration wanted to hear about
it. Ed Gray, a former public relations man for a California
thrift who had the misfortune to head the Federal Home
Loan Bank Board, had supported Garn-St. Germain but felt
he had to speak out about the legalized fraud routinely
taking place across the nation. Secretary of the Treasury
Donald Regan, the former head of Merrill Lynch, which specialized in the kind of brokered deposits now flowing into
and bankrupting the nation's thrifts, was furious with Gray,
saying he was "off the reservation" and not a team player.
Brokered deposits into thrifts had increased tenfold from
late 1981 to late 1983, and Gray, also called a "Nazi" because he wanted to bring order to this chaos, was desperately
trying to limit the percentage of brokered deposits a thrift
could accept. At the same time, legislators with friends running thrifts were constantly calling Gray to help them out of
jams with the regulators—who were hardly all that threatening. Deregulation had reduced their ranks, and their
morale and salaries were low and turnover high. So the
money from savings and loans kept right on being borrowed
and spent on the fantastic whims of its borrowers. By 1986,*

*the* FSLIC *had* two and a half billion on hand to cover deposits of $800 billion *in 3,249 savings and loans.*

*Gray's attempt in 1984 to limit brokered deposits was blocked by the courts, and it was not until 1987 that Congress allowed the bank board to raise $10.8 billion to rescue dying thrifts. The wholesale fraud was hardly an issue in the 1988 election, although curiously enough, the day after George Bush won the White House, regulators issued orders to seize Silverado Savings and Loan, where Bush's son, Neil, was on the board of directors that had approved millions in bad loans; known as "Desperado," when it failed Silverado would cost American taxpayers* $1 billion, *an amount Neil Bush called "inconsequential." In December 1988, the bank board secretly sold off seventy-five dying thrifts, and two weeks after Bush was sworn in, the new administration came up with a bailout plan and the creation of the Resolution Trust Corporation (*RTC*), a complicated bureaucracy that would take over and sell off the insolvent thrifts and which the* FDIC *Chairman has called "the biggest liquidation in the history of the world"—but that is another story. In 1989, having been kept alive for seven years at snowballing costs to the taxpayer, the vast majority of thrifts went under.*

*The largest amounts of money were lost in California. Money was poured into projects like the $150 million Phoenician Hotel in the Arizona desert, which would have had to be 70 percent occupied at five hundred dollars a night to make money, but for the most part California wheeled and dealed on paper. Like the gambler who has lost so much that his only chance is to stay at the table and win it all back, California thrifts began betting their deposits on interest rate swings and pouring their money into junk bonds, many of which were sold to elderly people who thought they*

*were insured. But it was in Texas, where sixty-five thrifts*
*failed to California's fourteen, that a physical transforma-*
*tion of the landscape took place.*

*Former real estate developers owned more than 80 per-*
*cent of the thrifts that failed in the Lone Star State, and they*
*expressed their visions of themselves in immense architec-*
*tures of a style that became almost national—even in New*
*Haven, where I had moved, a red-clay stone and money-*
*green reflective-glass office complex sat in postmodern*
*splendor beside the harbor, recalling the adobe and blue sky*
*of the Southwest. No, no state could match the audacity of*
*Texas in the s&l years. The every-man-for-himself philoso-*
*phy was so entrenched there that those who came into con-*
*tact with savings and loan money seemed to lose all sense of*
*reality or morality or reason. A Texas real estate salesperson*
*remembered a closing in the hall of an office building, where*
*investors were lined up at tables. "The loan officers would*
*close one sale and pass the papers to the next guy. It looked*
*like kids registering for college. If any investor raised a ques-*
*tion, someone would come over and tell them to leave, they*
*were out of the deal." At the end of all this buying and flip-*
*ping, enormous loans would be taken out on the now-*
*inflated properties. When Vernon Savings and Loan, one of*
*the most deposit swollen s&ls in Texas, finally failed, an*
*incredible* 96 percent of its outstanding loans were bad.

*Dallas was the site of some of the worst overbuilding,*
*and when I left the city I headed north, past the useless con-*
*struction frenzy that had haunted Ed Gray as early as 1983.*
*Past the architect-designed suburban corporate campuses*
*in Plano, Texas became a land of long horizons and pickup*
*trucks; here and there, a developer late getting into the ac-*
*tion had incongruously started housing subdivisions that*
*were later abandoned. Further north along the hundred or so*

miles to the state line there were gentle green hills through which snaked low-lying creeks and rivers; cows shifted their stance behind fences in various states of repair.

All the way to Oklahoma! was the cry of Dallas developers before it all came crashing down.

All the way to Oklahoma!

# Reflections in a Mirror-Skin Building

All-day parking in downtown Dallas can cost as little
as seventy-five cents, a bargain, in an area of more than
3.5 million, revealing how much of the city's downtown was demolished and made into parking lots
in the feverish land grab that reached its peak in the
1980s. Most of the nineteenth-century houses are
gone, along with the tan-brick office buildings of the
1920s. A commercial red-brick section called the West
End was saved from the wrecking ball, however, and
it now has little bistros and horsedrawn carts, and
people can come to see this remaining piece of the
Dallas past as a tourist attraction. It is a past disconnected—one might even say completely marginalized—
and to stand in the quiet sunshine of downtown Dallas
is to feel at the bottom of things, not at the center of a
powerful city but at its hollowed-out core. There are
only some 230 housing units here; and aside from the
endless stream of tourists heading for the sixth floor of
the Texas School Book Depository, the area's human
life consists mostly of a diurnal flow of office workers
in and out of the soaring office towers a few blocks
north.

These, of course, are the monuments to commerce
that today dominate the skyline, with marble plazas
and fountains and sleek glass doors opening into magnificent lobbies that suggest stable, established financial firms. Skyscrapers like the First Interstate Bank
Tower, with its pinnacled peak, or the seventy-story
NationsBank Building, outlined at night in green

argon, were created in a time when building cranes
were likened to birds in downtown Dallas, the bright
hammering of construction the happy song of a thriving metropolis. But many of these were built for banks
that no longer exist. Dallas lost almost all its original
banks in the 1980s as they failed and were bought out
by larger ones in an effort to keep faith in the system;
RepublicBank, for instance, had been a Texas institu-
tion before taxpayers bailed it out for some $6 billion.
Across from Ross Perot's Meyersohn Symphony Hall,
the concrete supports for yet another high-rise suggest
how completely construction has been stilled. Below
them, an extensive underground parking garage represents an investment no developer would walk away
from, but no office tower will be built. In 1993,
Cushman and Wakefield estimated that some 39
percent of downtown offices were vacant.

The centers of cities have been abandoned all over
the country, but especially in Texas, where the feder-
ally encouraged market forces in the Sun Belt joined
hands with the money lent out by banks and thrifts.
This supply of money, rather than population or business growth, drove the market, which finally collapsed
under the weight of too many buildings and not
enough people or businesses to lease or buy them. The
economic boom propped up by money from the savings and loan industry was embraced with a stunning
fervor in Dallas, which, trying to overcome John F.
Kennedy's assassination, had reveled, in the 1970s, in
the forward-looking vision of the airport.

Indeed, Dallas-Fort Worth International (DFW) em-
ploys some 35,000 people; the world's largest airport,
it is the second busiest after Chicago's O'Hare. Man-
dated by the Federal Aviation Administration in the

mid-1960s, it merged the once-separate cities of Dallas
and Fort Worth into a "metroplex"—a name that un-
derscores the technological and monolithic construction grid imposed on the area—and lured corporate
businesses in droves. Crucial for the shipment of
goods, the airport keeps businesspeople only a few
hours from anyplace in the country, and its central
time zone maximizes the hours of the business day on
both coasts. Scores of high-profile corporations and
some 1,100 companies with assets over $1 million
have come to take advantage of the "right-to-work
laws, favorable tax systems, and responsive governments" that marketing brochures extol; and perhaps
Dallas, straddling the Trinity River, was slated for such
a fate. The city was never about anything as dirty and
earth-bound as oil. Settled by artisans who abandoned
Charles Fourier's nearby utopian La Réunion community and its idealistic notions of social harmony and
organized agriculture, Dallas prospered by speculation. John Neely Bryan, who sold liquor, food, and
guns to westward-bound pioneers and housing lots to
those who were tired of the journey, was the first in a
long line of entrepreneurial gamblers, many of whom
profited handsomely by investing in land around the
railroads. After shipping and the railroads declined,
speculation around the transportation infrastructure
continued to shape the city. The airport and the freeway made modern-day Dallas, brought it into the
global age and opened up its immense, flat, outlying
lands for development.

When this history collided with the free-flowing
money in 1980s, Dallas became a financial and real-
estate mecca, an identity the city embraced so eagerly
that half the downtown's pre–World War II buildings,

and whatever they meant in terms of continuity and a sense of place, were destroyed to make way for the big deals; developers found the income from parking lots preferable to paying taxes on old buildings. As the city was redeveloped toward the north with "Other People's Money" (which was really the American tax-payers'), sleepy little areas found themselves doubling and tripling in population, building houses and office space and huge malls; infrastructure for these ventures gobbled up much of the city budget. City services regularly favored the northward expansion at the expense of South and East and West Dallas, where people had darker skin or the land was sometimes flooded by the Trinity or was too industrialized; the disparity in proportionment of city funds became so extreme that the southern Dallas community of Oak Cliff threatened to secede. Nevertheless, in the 1980s, the area around the northerly Galleria Mall became the new unofficial downtown, perpetuating the racial segregation that has long shaped the city. Along the Dallas North Tollway, the landscape became a show-place for the empty speculative failures known as see-through buildings. Blanketed with shopping malls and suburban home developments, defined by corpo-rate office ventures, Dallas is a spectacular example of how a region can be transformed, in as little as twenty years, into a particular kind of built environment, a conglomeration of irrevocable structures only margin-ally connected to the public good.

The sense of the area's manipulated social structure first came to me not long after I dropped off the car with the valet at Las Colinas, a twelve-thousand-acre office and residential complex that was my first stop in Dallas-Fort Worth. Billing itself as "America's Corporate Headquarters," Las Colinas is the brainchild of Texas developer Ben Carpenter, who, seeing that his family's cattle ranch sat alongside the future site of DFW, decided to turn the land into a private world for business. One of the country's first "master-planned communities," and today the regional or national home of companies like Exxon, TRW, and GTE, it is a world of clean roads and massive modern structures that seem to rise from nowhere on the north Texas plain. Some fifty thousand people work in Las Colinas and some twenty thousand live there in luxury homes and upscale apartments, enjoying the restaurants, country clubs, hotels, shops, banks, spa, sports club, and five thousand acres of open space. Carpenter also created placid lakes and waterways to guard against flooding. In this and other ways the reconfigured land is reminiscent of Disney World, an ahistorical, private, prefabricated, and completely controlled world, the product of a plan to eliminate the unpleasant aspects of public life through financial and social exclusion.

That tens of thousands of area workers began commuting to Las Colinas was a blow to downtown Dallas, but the young man from Las Colinas marketing was candid about the development's lack of concern for the city center. We were standing on the top floor of a postmodern high-rise on Williams Square in Las Colinas, looking through picture windows at a wraparound view of the Dallas-Fort Worth area; the sense of dominion over the land was underscored by a scale model of Las Colinas in the center of the room. It was the first time I had ever been in a private city, inorganic and planned from above, and as the marketing man kept extolling the development's elaborate and technologically sophisticated security, I remarked quite pleasantly that what it really seemed to be about was class segregation.

"You could call it that," he smiled, as if we were in on a little joke together.

Back at the Holiday Inn in downtown Dallas I tried to buy a comb and a notebook. The only place open was a little ethnic grocery store that didn't sell them, and the woman at the hotel desk finally clued me in to the fact that all the shops were in underground walkways beneath the streets.

"There's a CVS down there and everything," she said, looking at her watch, "but you just missed it. They close at six. They're really for the people in the office buildings, and most everybody's gone home by now." She handed me a visitor's map on which the underground streets and an accompanying system of skywalks made an impressive, brightly colored grid. "That's where the real city is," a librarian told me the next morning, describing cafés and restaurants and little shops that made it all sound cosmopolitan and exciting.

Although it struck me as a complication not just to have stores right on the street, the next day I entered the NationsBank Building and floated down the escalator. Everything seemed immediately familiar. It was an enclosed, intensified world of chrome, potted plants, and glibly cheerful neon, configured to extract the maximum consumer dollars: a mall, that's all.

"What are these underground walkways *for*?" I asked a guard. "Security," he said, and then looked at me strangely—why didn't I know?

But downtown Dallas was too sleepy to be really frightening, and two-tiered cities are historically rare. The medieval English town of Chester built an over-ground system of walkways because of periodic flooding; a more ambitious effort, impelled by social rather than geographic concerns, was built in Florence in 1565, when the Medicis erected the covered world of the Ponte Vecchio to insulate themselves from the smells and chaos of Florentine life. In our time, however, the multilevel city is linked with corporate capital. The international trading center of Hong Kong, for instance, has an elaborate system of skywalks, and cities like Montreal, Calgary, Detroit, Minneapolis, Houston, and Denver have built underground walkways and overhead bridges. The appearance of the tiered city in North America, at a time of concentrated private wealth alongside homelessness, AIDS, and other street-level urban problems, suggests that these walkways also spring from an insular worldview. In Dallas, said to have the third-largest concentration of corporate headquarters in the United States, this walkway system is highly developed: The relocation of foot traffic in the downtown has been very successful.

The old downtowns of what some critics, planners, and architects have dismissively described as nineteenth-century cities—as if they are passé and no longer adequate, a concept Europeans must find remarkable—were more independently arranged hodge-podges of small businesses than these subterranean malls; a business renting space negotiated with a landlord who owned the building, and only sometimes the whole block; some businesses themselves owned the building. If a neighborhood became trendier, landlords could charge more, but over time. In malls, however, a single management authority controls the composition of hundreds of stores at once, constantly changing the mixture of retailers to boost overall mall productivity. Curfewed, controlled, and dedicated to sophisticated marketing techniques, enclosed retail realms are not, like the streets of downtown cities, public spaces. The underground walkways in Dallas will never be the site of political demonstrations, homeless people, begging, or other signs of social unrest or injustice, and musicians, oddballs, marginal artists, and the other colorful bit players of an open society have also been excised by a strange surgery that gives the illusion of a clean and prosperous public life. Weather has been used to justify walkways from Calgary to Dallas, in areas where people have always shopped and congregated, but "under the guise of convenience," one critic has noted, "we are imposing a middle-class tyranny" on the once-respected centers of nonconformity and tolerance and the arts.

I felt no need to explore the skywalks.

Joel Barna, author of an excellent study of 1980s Texas building, *The See-Through Years*, argues that the frantic real estate market—whose collapse caused an estimated one million Texans to lose their homes in half a decade—was fueled by the widely held belief that developers were ordained princes who would bring prosperity to all. As if in physical confirmation of this idea, the gateway to the remarkable overbuilding along the elevated Dallas North Tollway is a giant medieval castle parked right next to the highway. This is the $90 million Providence Towers, a red-granite and bronze-tinted glass office extravaganza with a huge multistory arch cut in the middle of it. Only 45 per-

cent occupied until 1992, it sums up a number of
building attitudes and truths that held sway here in
the 1980s—that granite suggests stability, that tinted
or reflective glass is cheap, and that office buildings offer the highest potential investment return. It is also
the grim embodiment of an American fantasy aesthetic, clearly symbolic of the delusions of grandeur
that built this landscape.

Just past it the failed savings and loan monoliths
begin. For miles at a time, huge geometric structures
flank the high, lanes-wide tollway, and too many of
the giant shapes are skinned with impenetrable mirrors, overseeing the road like the reflecting sunglasses
of a hostile patrolman. Trees or flowers or fountains
might soften them at street level, but from the tollway
the entire landscape, with its multistory parking
garages, electrical pylons, mirrors, towers, and enormous malls, is an awesome product of the machine.
It has the aching glare of an acid trip, built though it
was for a middle-class and corporate clientele.

On a weekday afternoon the parking lots suggested
the vacancy rates. A blocky red-granite building with
round windows for a defunct Texas thrift—empty. The
building housing J. C. Penney's offices before it completed its corporate villa up in Plano—empty. A high-
rise apartment tower with a Mediterranean motif—
never finished. A massive shopping center spread out
behind a vacant parking lot—For Lease, Available
Now, Inquire Within. Going on and on, these mam-
moth buildings were often sold by the Resolution
Trust Corporation for dimes and quarters and change
on the dollar. Many were thrown up so fast, using such
shoddy construction, that they had to be reskinned
after only a few years, when their glass panels began

falling off—but nothing mattered so much as completing those buildings and making those fortunes. Tax-
devalued empty office space in many American cities
became as accepted a feature of urban life in the early
1990s as the homelessness booming at the same
time; its visual impact was just far more exaggerated
in Dallas.

Despite its nightmarish side, however, which apparently seems normal to many people, newly developed North Dallas is the most fashionable part of
town. Neiman Marcus, Saks, gourmet shops, exotic
restaurants, and expensive boutiques—the shopping
for the well-to-do is concentrated there in the malls.
Off the freeway, North Dallas is like any thriving "edge
city," "exopolis," "urban node," or whatever the latest
suburban sprawl might be called: huge malls, multi-
lane streets, dedicated turning lanes, traffic jams. The
big department stores will not go to historic Main
Street shopping districts, which are regarded as sec-
ond-rate and often stay alive through redevelopment
grants and other public incentives. A city planner I
spoke to agreed that in Dallas new is simply seen as
better. Although the Big D is as old as San Francisco,
"it's a young city" was the justification I heard frequently for the all-out embrace of the new, as if the
reasons behind it were social and cultural, and not the
product of immense economic forces allowed to run
wild.

Past the monoliths, new housing subdivisions form
a sea of chimneys and steeply pitched roofs floating in
the heat, walled and set back from the highway. Also
appealing to the love of the new, suggesting security
from declines in value with their restrictive covenants,

the big brick houses of North Dallas appear to be of good quality. For renters, however, clusters of apartment complexes—Glens and Meadows and Parks and Estates—are made from cheaper materials, because after twelve or twenty years or so they'll be treated as teardowns. My guide, an architect active in historic preservation, had lost his ability to be stunned by the disposability of Dallas architecture, but that concept of disposability, cornerstone of consumer culture, was in fact an unmistakable undercurrent in the city. It extended not only to things and buildings but even to the downtown urban way of life, where people walked and saw the past and came together with different social classes, a way of life the man at Las Colinas saw as an anachronism. The logical extreme of this disposability was the American taxpayers' money, and on the way there it engulfed the North Dallas landscape as if it were nothing more, as Barna put it, than a blank canvas on which to sketch wildly ambitious marketing ideas. Aside from demonstrating how completely the concept of an organized built environment was given up in the city, the Dallas North Tollway represents an almost unfathomable anarchy of investment. This distended monument to moral and social failure is the permanent brand of an era when public money that could have bought education, health care, parks, libraries, and other human decencies financed a total surrender to colossal greed.

A day or so later another preservationist was telling me about the Federal General Services Administration's plans to build a three-block, low-rise office campus amid all that empty office space in downtown Dallas.

"I'm sure it's just stupidity," she said, part of a anti-government chorus I heard over and over in Dallas.

She was showing me out when a fortyish, sandy-haired man, overweight and sweating from the heat, said hello. He wore a black polo shirt, a gold earring, and an overly optimistic air. "I feel like home sales might finally pick up again in North Dallas," he said, soon rhapsodizing about the boom days. He claimed that he and another businessman had made a bid for the famously troubled Centrum Building, only to have the Resolution Trust Corporation nix the deal and end up selling it for $7 million less a year later. Sketching a map to lots he was selling in North Dallas, he strongly advised me to take a look. "The lots in Las Flores are going for two hundred thousand to seven hundred thousand for a half acre," he said, mopping his brow, "and the ones at the Downs at Hilltop are going for between one hundred and two hundred seventy-five, but they're a bit smaller."

For less than half an acre?

"Sure, you know why? Water. There are lakes on these properties, and so they're always going to be expensive." He leaned back as if he'd given me a big tip—although I was thinking he'd misused the word *lake* and needed *pond*.

Man-made lakes?

"Oh, sure, most of the lakes around here are man-made. There's also a lot of old houses from the thirties and forties we're treating as teardowns." He circled another area on his map.

The woman and I went outside. "I never know whether to believe him or not," she said tactfully as we crossed the street. "But people did become million-aires overnight. A woman I knew in Highland Park sold her house by naming the first figure that came to mind, which was a million dollars. Of course, the developer who bought it filed for Chapter 11," she added, as I envisioned him borrowing the funds from a bank or thrift.

We were standing by a large grassy lot shaded by trees. "Over there, that's the Centrum you just heard about." She gestured past the grass, just as a waitress from a trendy Tex-Mex restaurant across the street walked up.

"Do you want to know about this lot?" the waitress asked.

"No, I'm just pointing out a few things," the preservationist said.

"Oh," the waitress replied. "I thought you were looking at the lot. It belongs to the owner of the restaurant, and he wants to sell, or if he can't sell it pretty soon turn it into a parking lot. I thought you might be interested."

By 1986, the time had passed for any real planning in North Dallas, and as I turned off an upscale commercial strip to visit the earring-millionaire's North Dallas homesites, the immediate switch from franchise chains to exclusive developments was astonishing. At the turn-in to Las Flores a uniformed guard emerged from a landscaped and substantial entrance house. I signed some papers, the electronic gates opened, and I drove onto a site that seemed more like a marketing fantasy than a development. The "waterfalls and spillways" were only about two feet wide. The manorlike homes, vaguely Newport and Beaux Arts in feeling, were huge but unnaturally close together, and only four of the twenty-two lots had been sold.

Nearby, clusters of independent developments occupied various upper rungs of the social ladder. Next door to Las Flores, large ranch houses were pleasantly landscaped with azaleas and generous front lawns on streets that were still public rights-of-way. Across the avenue, flashy new cars sat outside brick houses set in tight culs-de-sac, with brick driveways, brick mailboxes, even brick landscape edging—a neat, maintenance-free way to build as many homes as possible on a small parcel. At the Downs at Hilltop, the land, still strewn with equipment and bare spots, showed the effects of being endlessly moved around by bulldozers, and the houses were ostentatious and elaborate, with slate roofs, gables, skylights, and towers. Farther north, past expensive subdivisions identical to those in Denver and Phoenix and scores of other cities, there were endless streets of brick North Dallas "specials" with their luxurious fireplaces, kitchens, and high ceilings, sometimes only ten feet from each other, often with back alleyways not so much for parking as to separate visitors by social function and cut down on taxable land. These long miles of expensive housing in North Dallas—with pockets of cluster apartments in the same static, grass-clipped mode—express a collective fantasy of American development seen in communities from Florida to California, a neat, clean world of property owners and tamed tracts of nature, a seamless consumer culture without past, poverty, or idiosyncrasy.

As these houses were erected in the north, existing houses for the less moneyed were razed for development closer to downtown. The Vineyard, a residential neighborhood of Victorian and Prairie-style wooden homes, was decimated by arson following a huge corporation's stealthy buy-up of the area. Elsewhere, eighty-one acres of an African American community were cleared for development. One of the most dramatic clearings took place near Southland Corporation's CityPlace development, proposed in 1983. This ambitious project was to contain luxury condos, apartments, a hotel, a shopping center, and a greenbelt, anchored by twin office towers that would frame the North Central Expressway as a "gateway to downtown Dallas." Southland, of 7-Eleven fame, secretly assembled 150 acres of surrounding land and demolished hundreds of single-family homes and modest office and apartment buildings. Southland did replace some of that housing, but only one of the two planned towers was built, and it was for years an empty and ghostly tower; still, it has four kinds of marble on the floor and African mahogany on the walls. Outside, the Haskell Mall, a six-lane boulevard with granite curbs, brick sidewalks, and hundreds of trees, represents an ultimately unnecessary $20 million public investment— in stark contrast to street after West Dallas street, in the classic picture of Southern poverty, that still hadn't gotten curbs or sidewalks from the city.

When I first drove into one of the cleared areas, I didn't realize what it was. It seemed an innocuous stretch of parkland, flat and grassy, dotted with lovely and eccentric old trees. But the sidewalks and driveway openings marked this as a former residential area. It was ghostly, thinking about all those people who had been moved out, and I could not understand why the trees remained standing, why a developer who could uproot an entire community would bother saving trees. Later I asked around and learned that the answer was economic. Bulldozing structures is one phase of a clearing operation. But it doesn't make financial

sense to pay a tree surgeon until you know what
you're going to do with the property. So when
CityPlace stopped, one tower left alone in an empty
world, the people were gone but the trees remained.

Dallas had always been about speculation, but the
overbuilding and the wholesale capitulation to the
forces that physically moved the city really took off in
1976. In that year a plan to restrict northern growth to
areas that could be served by mass transit was laid to
rest by the narrow election to mayor of developer
Robert Folsom, later sued for $30 million by Bank
One, at the time preoccupied with the Bent Tree Office
Towers that he ultimately lost to the RTC. A lot of
players went bankrupt in the late 1980s and were
counted out, but like any gambling game, North
Dallas real estate fostered addicts. According to the
*Dallas Business Journal*, people instrumental in the financial collapse of the 1980s picked up properties at
bargain prices from the RTC even though they still
owed millions to banks and thrifts taken over by the
Feds. They became hooked on the deal as an end in itself, a personal quest for riches. The people left out of
the action brought lawsuits, of course, and the threats
of secession; and after the real estate market collapse,
the system that had prevented anything resembling
an equitable distribution of funds was dented. But
even after all those thrift and bank failures and all
those useless buildings, an endless mantra of develop,
develop, develop is heard daily in Dallas. "It's not
pretty, or sensitive," a building official said of the political situation. "Politicians always run on campaigns
of no new taxes." The mentality of ruthlessness and
I've-got-mine still dominates, and the physical built

reality in Dallas is overwhelming, indisputable, permanent.

One of the few landholders with the ability to make long-range investments and wait for the right opportunity, Ross Perot made a lot of money in the northern Dallas suburb of Plano. He used to own 2,300 acres of the Legacy Park development that houses the Frito Lay and Electronic Data Systems headquarters. As of 1993, the Perot Group owned twenty-six miles of interstate frontage—25,000 clean-slate acres—along I-35 north of Fort Worth, a more western city of rodeos and railroads that largely escaped the destruction and overbuilding of the 1980s.

Perot's plans for those acres revolve around the Alliance Airport northwest of DFW. Some years ago the Federal Aviation Administration asked Perot to donate land for a small reliever airport for DFW, not unlike a number of them already ringing the region. The FAA had a ten-year horizon for the project, but Perot's son, Ross Jr., approached General Dynamics, Bell Helicopter, and other area electronic and aerospace firms and asked if they could use a high-tech commercial airport fifteen miles from DFW. When they said yes, the Perot Group told the FAA they would like to see an airport on the land, but something bigger, to serve as an economic development tool. The FAA was not initially receptive to the idea. But then Fort Worth Congressman and Speaker of the House Jim Wright, later to accept a campaign contribution from Perot and to resign his post after an ethics committee accused him of sixty-nine violations of House rules including accepting inappropriate gifts from a Fort

Worth developer, was invited to view the proposed
project from a Perot helicopter. Construction began
in eighteen months, and Alliance Airport opened
eighteen months later. Perot also managed to get
$200 million in tax breaks, more than double the ap-
propriation given to O'Hare, the nation's largest passenger airport, and, in one year, some three and a half
times the funds reliever airports usually receive.

The second largest airport in North Texas after
DFW, supersophisticated technologically, Alliance
Airport can handle all existing transport aircraft and is
operated twenty-four hours a day by the FAA. While
publicly owned by the City of Fort Worth, it is the
key to Perot's surrounding Alliance developments.
Alliance Center is a business and industrial park that
has attracted Ishida Aerospace Research, the Drug
Enforcement Agency's Aviation Support Headquarters,
and American Airlines maintenance operations, this
last after Ross Jr. personally lobbied legislators in
Austin to grant a $50 million property tax reduction
over fifteen years. Alliance Gateway, another Perot development, houses distribution facilities for Nestlé
and Food Lion, with rail lines leading right into the
warehouse. As a third aspect of the venture, Perot is
developing Park Glen, a $1,100-acre subdivision south
of the airport, with homes from the $70s to the
$170s—available employee housing helps attract com-
panies to the area. At "peak development," according
to brochures, it is hoped that 163,000 jobs will be created at Alliance as industries relocate to take advantage of the North American Free Trade Agreement, the
right-to-work laws, and the government incentives for
business. Perot's tremendous economic force in the
area suggests that Fort Worth, although surely not as

audaciously, will be developed along the same lines as Dallas.

Ross Perot may have the largest role in shaping northern Fort Worth, but he is not the only major player moving into the rural lands north and west of DFW. Nearby, in conjunction with IBM, McGuire-Thomas Partners, which has billed itself as the number one developer in the country, has built a corporate park called Solana that is beautifully integrated into the landscape. Mexican-inspired architecture makes Solana seem distinctly international, and it is as simple and tasteful as Las Colinas is garish and self-important. And, in fact, the marketing people I met at these three different places reflected distinct corporate attitudes and visions. The young man at Las Colinas, confiding that he was soon to make his fortune in a home development venture, was convinced of his superiority to others less fortunate and unconnected to the corporate money machine. The immaculately groomed and gung-ho young Texan from the Perot Group believed as if in religion that if you had a good product like Alliance and could "market the hell out of it," success would follow. The intelligent and urbane man from McGuire-Thomas, acknowledging that a huge social responsibility has fallen on the developer, represented a post-1980s attitude. McGuire-Thomas has built a humane work environment with a focus on worker health and well-being, and the company even likes the fact that strip commercial development of the airport highway from DFW to Solana has been restricted by the local township.

But as Joel Barna has noted, there is something paternalistic, even feudal, about these developments: "The princes of the market have worked out the arrangements necessary for the worker's future, and everybody lives happily after." The development people all shared the feeling that they had the right to determine the built structures of the public's cities and rural areas, to fix the location of their jobs and houses, to influence public education through programs like Texas Scholars and Adopt-a-School so as to guarantee a useful labor force. The private sector is even working on the construction of roads. The Perot Group donated hundreds of acres toward the right-of-way for a highway linking Alliance to DFW, and then lobbied the government indefatigably for financing, tens of millions of which will come from the Federal Highway Commission and the State of Texas. In the area around Dallas-Fort Worth, business is accepted as an unquestionably positive force, as the church once was elsewhere; the term *market forces* has about it an air of divine inevitability—not something that could be directed and shaped toward the public's wishes. And indeed, the landscape and architecture of the entire region suggest a diminished public role.

That the private sector will continue to shape the physical and emotional landscape of the Dallas-Fort Worth area seems obvious. The gradual ceding of such traditionally public realms as transportation—a way to direct the growth of business because infrastructure is vital to the movement of people and goods—and education, through which people might imagine worlds beyond the corporate structure, will help guarantee it. Since the 1960s, corporations have been settling in increasingly more isolated and controlled environments and will continue to do so. This will ensure that jobs will be introduced, not to alleviate unemployment, but to take advantage of educated labor bases in the classic pattern of class and racial segregation. The corporate wisdom that social problems can be dealt with through security and class separation has clearly prevailed in the metroplex. The public good has been so equated with the good of business in the North Dallas-Fort Worth area that to travel it is to feel heavy with the sense that the public has abandoned its powers of self-determination.

There is no lack of ideas for what might be done in Dallas, but city planners, at the mercy of dwindling funds, overwhelmed by recurrent crises and neighborhood issues, have not been able to make long-term planning a priority. Architect James Pratt proposed and publicized a humane and imaginative plan to diversify housing and transportation and use river meanders, bluffs, and other topographic features to create public amenities, but it did not have a price tag—not that a price tag was at all its point. The city council recently hired the consultant services of the Dallas Plan, funded by a civic-minded businessman, naturally, to elicit public participation and perform the rational task of formulating major capital improvement strategy. But little can really be done about the fact that the city has a monolithic, low-density, car-oriented built environment with a diminished sense of the past, and its daily physical presence and its immense costs in terms of sewage, water, roads, and other infrastructure pose a formidable obstacle to thinking about the city in ways that go beyond its use as a development site for business. A north Texas economist who shall mercifully go uncited said at a 1991 symposium that "perhaps the best hope for downtown might be to turn it into a theme park, with a major public attraction in each of its quadrants." The language of this

degraded notion of possibility reflects a vision of land
and place and public activity far removed from civic or
cosmopolitan progress. Or perhaps the speaker had
simply conflated all public gatherings for enrichment
with the crass commercialism and intellectual vacu-
ousness of the theme park, revealing how casually the
citizen is seen as nothing more than a consumer or a
child to be entertained.

The JFK Museum in Dallas, called "The Sixth Floor" after its location in the Texas School Book Depository, is
free, and like a passageway to another reality, an elevator whisks people up and down all day long. It's an intelligent and thoughtful place, with photographs of
the books, TV shows, and crazes from 1963, as well as
background on the conservative Dallas political
groups that worried Kennedy's security team. By the
time the stilled, familiar pictures of the open black
convertibles in Dealey Plaza began to appear, I could
hear people weeping just ahead; as the cars moved in
photographs toward inevitable tragedy, a low-tuned,
original audio broadcast, anachronistic with clunky
authority, provided a reliving of its aftermath. There
was an exhibit on the Warren Commission, and then
a video began reporting that "the American people
continued to have doubts" about the shooting, describing the grassy knoll, the dead witnesses, the extra
bullets. A further film was also available for viewing,
and near the exit there was a blank open register
where visitors were asked to record their feelings so
that future historians could better understand the sig-
nificance of the event.

    After all I had seen in Dallas, I had expected presi-
dential seals and flags, a preconceived thesis, more

glitter and hype and heavily moneyed hands at work, and "The Sixth Floor," with its toned-down name and assertion that the opinions of ordinary people had meaning and value, struck me as an anomaly in the area. Surely this was a result of the unique nature of the assassination itself, which abruptly ended an American innocence whose loss was ultimately too profound to be tampered with. But it was also because, like any piece of expression that moves minds, the museum represented something greater than itself. It represented the loss of one of the last moments in memory when people still believed in government as a force of good to shape their lives, and the weeping revealed how really painful Americans have found the loss of that trust. And afterward there was nothing that embodied some human part of ourselves to offer that trust to. After Vietnam and Watergate and the hostages in Tehran there was only a man who made a show of offering deliverance. And he said, I understand that you don't believe in government anymore, but you don't even have to. All you have to believe in is business.

Modern-day Dallas, of course, marks the physical realization of that idea.

# A Clouding Over
## of the Blue-Sky Dream

*Completing its line into Los Angeles in 1885, the Santa Fe Railroad wasted no time before engaging in a rate war with the Southern Pacific that is said to have Americanized California. Passenger fares from Kansas City to the coast sank to one dollar, but it was worth bringing people out there because men like Thomas A. Scott of the Pennsylvania Railroad, who had already bought up most of Ventura County at sixty-five cents an acre, planned to make a lot of money selling land. In many cases their holdings were so vast that land and water companies had to be created to sell them, and in the spirit of P.T. Barnum and Buffalo Bill Cody their salesmen were likely to say, "Let us have our stage-coach drivers meeting these Easterners sport big sombreros and brandish blacksnake whips, and let us build a hotel, so that our visitors may rest in comfort." Buyers might also have surrey rides and picnics in the valleys before actually going out to see the lots.*

*In the 1920s another real estate boom hit, spurred by the discovery of in-ground petroleum. This one scattered little metal oil derricks across the blinking bright landscape, and the spoke-wheeled upright boxes of mass-produced automobiles jounced over the region's rutted roads. And after World War II there was yet another boom as the aerospace, defense, and high tech industries of John Kennedy's "new frontier" brought good jobs and the conveniences of the atomic age to southern California.*

*Following the same gridded logic that governed American land sales in the nineteenth century, the suburban tract*

*developments for this latest wave of white settlers were awe-
some mass-production projects, built, as the postwar apartment complexes of the communist countries were, for a mass
society whose qualifying members were seen as having indistinguishable needs and desires. Row after identical row of
homes were laid out on the flat former farmland, each with
the same architecture and the same lot and the same angle to
the sun as its neighbors. Photographs taken at various stages
of construction of, say, Lakewood, California, show the
bare leveled earth, then the demarcated lots with their individual electrical poles neatly spaced, then the cinder-block
foundation pads, the wooden frames, the plywood shells,
and finally the finished homes all lawned and ready. And
decade after decade more of them were built as if there could
never be enough.*

*But by the early 1990s the Golden State had become
overdeveloped, swollen with 31.5 million people, and in
southern California especially, it was becoming increasingly
hard to really appreciate the beauty of the West. The once-
new houses set amid spectacular scenery and the shopping
plazas built for them and the gas stations and roads to connect them had become so numerous that there was less and
less physical beauty to see. With a hundred and fifty bad air
days a year, the region often seems coated in a sad, silty,
automobile-produced grime; and even a study by the establishment Bank of America had to concede that "unchecked
sprawl has shifted from an engine of California's growth to
a force that now threatens to inhibit and degrade the quality
of life."*

*Then, too, the state's economy has been declining. With
defense industry downsizing at the end of the Cold War,
California lost 750,000 jobs in three years, more than
400,000 of them in Los Angeles County, and the region began to appeal only to those willing to take the low-wage ser-*

*vice jobs left behind. In 1992,* Newsweek *reported that up to 90 percent of California's newcomers were immigrants or children born to them, and the governor's office estimated that they cost $5 billion more in taxes each year than they brought in. By 1993, fewer than half of Los Angeles school-children were proficient in English, and the 1992 riots and the earthquake two years later underscored the feeling that California was a distinctly precarious place to be.*

*California is still building suburbs for affluent would-be buyers, however, gobbling up land, the American Farmland Trust reports, at the rate of an acre an hour. Curious about what subdivision dwellers in California might be thinking, I decided to visit one of the postwar suburbs in the sun.*

# In the Red Rock Valley
# of the Cowboy Westerns

"We have every right to dream heroic dreams," Ronald
Reagan stated simply in his first inaugural address, and
those words seem to float in the very air at his mission-
style presidential library set amid hills that served as
the backdrop for thousands of movie Westerns. From
the building's back esplanade it is possible, on a clear
day, to see across dry green hills dotted with gold and
magenta wildflowers more than thirty miles down to
the Pacific, and when the soft breezes moving in and
around the valley bring up the trill and chitter of birds
and squirrels, this view seems all that is breathtaking
and splendid about southern California. Inside, displays of Nancy's evening gowns and the famous White
House china and the gifts from foreign leaders in
carved ivory and gold and malachite and onyx link
the Reagan presidency to royal traditions of gift giving
and luxurious state dinners and so try to justify by
the centuries the highrolling tastes of the 1980s. But
the keys to Reagan's heroic dreams lie elsewhere, in
exhibits of Western art and artifacts like "Rawhide,"
in the celebration of ranching in "Ronald Reagan's
American West," in the displays of Reagan's saddles
and belts and Stetsons and spurs and gun belts, in the
oftrepeated idea that Reagan ended the Cold War—
indeed, in the whole idealized conception of the frontier man standing tall against the forces of savagery
and evil.

This library sits high above the community of Simi Valley, some forty-five minutes north of Los Angeles and a place that has for some years held the honor of being one of the safest cities of more than one hundred thousand in the nation. Made up almost entirely of subdivisions, it is a living museum of American Cold War suburban development. The central avenues that sprang up around the railroad feature those 1950s and 1960s cinder-block ranches with the mean and high little windows, and later the more spacious earth-toned and wood-shingled homes of the 1970s yielded to those boxy apartment complexes with the wood-railed balconies and one-side angled roofs. Now the luxurious pastel and red-tiled roof adobes of the developers' newest Southwest creep, in figurative and literal mobile ascension, up into the red rock hills that surround the valley. Amid the leisurely glinting traffic moving past the strip malls and gas-stationed intersections on the valley floor, each car heads its own way, for there is no historic downtown or central business district here. This is pure suburbia, and if by day the houses present their flat, two-car garage faces to the still and utterly empty street, after five there are joggers and hand-holding couples out for walks, homeowners watering their lawns or working on hobbies in open garages. The sunny bedroom community of Simi Valley has fulfilled for many the American dream of owning a home and a piece of land in beautiful country.

Yet it seemed, as I entered the modern, low-slung city hall on a pleasant March evening, that Simi Valley, home of the Rodney King verdict, laughingstock of the greater Los Angeles area for being a provincial and unimaginative community of tract homes, and the recent butt of jokes on *Saturday Night Live* and *NYPD Blue*, had once again suffered a national disgrace. On a recent trip to Washington, City Councilwoman Sandi Webb had, during a discussion of the right to carry firearms, directed profanities and an obscene gesture at the U.S. senator from California, Diane Feinstein. After three days of intense pressure Webb had finally apologized, but now, at a crowded city council meeting with TV cameras aimed and the National Rifle Association handing out speaker cards so that everyone could be "officially counted as favoring the right to carry," residents were taking the microphone to voice their outrage over the incident. "She has openly violated the law by carrying a concealed weapon," charged one; the meeting in Washington was a "disaster," declared another as half a dozen speakers came to the mike. "She is unfit to serve," came the last resounding declaration; the city council should "sanction and remove her."

Hearty boos, hisses, and some really loud coughing formed the immediate response from the audience, but the innocuous-looking Webb magnanimously waved her supporters off.

Some of the mike-takers had assailed Webb's stand on an earlier, controversial incident in which a man had taken a curious late night stroll in an unsavory part of the San Fernando Valley known as the "Zone." He had come upon a couple of graffiti taggers and was writing their descriptions in a notepad when they confronted him, possibly with screwdrivers. He pulled a gun and shot them, perhaps even as they were fleeing, and one died. Webb, a libertarian, had taken it upon herself to call the shooter a crime-fighting hero and to voice her support for him on National Public Radio. Now, at the council meeting, she moved on to the Feinstein incident.

"Ninety percent of the calls I received supported me," she said, "and I came to apologize on my own." At this there was an instant wave of applause, sustained clapping, and from some, even a standing ovation.

All this talk was leading straight into item 7A on the night's agenda, consideration of the state law regulating the carrying of concealed weapons. The local police had the authority to issue permits, and Police Chief Adams, described as "taking a conservative approach and no big brother," was out to make it easier for Simi residents to carry guns. He was going to broaden the "just cause" clause to include not only those who carried valuables or had received threats, but anyone who felt the need to carry a weapon, and he was going to make it possible to carry up to three pieces, in case one felt the need for weaponry at the shoulder, hip, and ankle. There was, however, a catch. He was requiring a psychological test and personal liability coverage of $1 million, mainly because a disturbed, rock-and-bottle-throwing resident had recently shot and killed a police officer coming to check on him at his neighbors' request. The audience, however, did not like that psychological testing idea one bit. "It implies that you're crazy if you want to defend yourself," one twelve-year resident who worked in the San Fernando Valley complained. He saw no reason why Simi should be the first to require such testing, and he felt that its cost, along with the extra insurance, amounted to a "poll tax" on those who wanted to carry.

Most of the people who got up to speak were not actually responding to the chief's proposal. They just wanted to stand up and state publicly that carrying a gun was not a privilege but a right outlined in the Constitution. That was why the National Rifle Association had stacked the meeting and that was why they were here. But during that evening I heard language that was to recur over and over during my days in Simi, refrains like "over the line," "over the boundary," "over the hill," and "outside the valley," all of which referred to the valley's geographic isolation in Ventura just over the Los Angeles County line and to its sense of separateness from the gang-ridden San Fernando Valley and the urban chaos of Los Angeles itself. The passionately reiterated need to defend one's life and property with a gun seemed odd given the city's famous reputation for safety, and the following day I told a local reporter that I had been astonished at the level of fear at that meeting.

"That wasn't fear," he told me easily. "Those weren't little old ladies getting up there—they were men. They aren't afraid. They're just defending a way of life."

Since the 1870s, Simi Valley had been primarily used for agriculture, and by 1960, when there were about eight thousand people in the valley, the economics of water brought about change. It was clear that it would have to be imported from Los Angeles, and farmers felt the cost would make their ventures unprofitable; some decided to sell. To the east, the San Fernando Valley was filling up, and developers began to tout Simi as "the valley of your future," playing on the new nearby rocket propulsion labs at North American Aviation, the Rocketdyne field lab, and the nuclear reactors being developed at Atomic International. It was possible, with the GI Bill, to buy a brand new house with just five hundred dollars or even nothing down, and if the valley's location without a freeway added a little risk to the venture, new homeowners could take inspiration from the high school football team, the "Pioneers." By 1965 the population of the Simi Valley had more than quintupled to forty-three thousand.

Simi attracted the white, Protestant, blue-collar families of policemen and firemen from L.A. County and factory workers from the General Motors plant and the aerospace industries in the San Fernando Valley. Its rapid growth brought a need to control billboards, build sidewalks, and consolidate water and sewer districts, and these led to the valley becoming a city in 1969, although the first vote for local government failed. The conservative Western ethos of less government was sufficiently strong, in fact, to cause bitter dissent in the new city. Meetings for sewer assessment districts—and everyone was assessed, whether they wanted to be or not—were downright hostile. There were death threats and vulgarities, and one council member was accused of being "an admitted world traveler"; the police had to escort the others to their cars. Even today, the city has no general fund property tax and is supported by license fees, sales tax, and taxes from businesses. But "this is no Orange County," a city official said; there have never been layoffs in City Hall, and Simi has a high-tech police department with new patrol cars. The city itself has become more upwardly mobile. Now it is largely the home of college-educated, white-collar office workers, and new homes have increasingly become more luxurious over the years.

When I crossed the Santa Susana Mountains that
gave way to the valley, I too had the sense of moving into a time and space completely distinct from
Los Angeles. Perched in those red rock hills, the
McDonald's on the freeway into town where I stopped
for coffee could have been in Arizona or the empty
Southwest; one of the main avenues in the valley was
lined with stately, well-established palms, suggesting
the time-stopped world of a desert oasis, and the air,
too, was no longer balmy. Indeed, a recent survey of
ten thousand residents revealed the pleasure people
took in Simi's "less hectic and crowded atmosphere,"
its "open, country-like feeling"; it suggested, too, that
residents saw it as a place that had so far escaped "the
big city woes of Los Angeles." It is a "haven that people have run to" as a kind of "last straw after being fed
up elsewhere." But the feeling of safety has come not
only from the geography but from the human imposi-
tion of law and order and authority. "A lot of LAPD
officers made their home here and it's been a community where people feel safe," a city official told me.
"This rest room is under surveillance," read a ladies'
room sign in McDonald's.

To be sure, the city was not entirely in order. There
were areas where the old cinder-block ranches had tall
grass in the yard or foil or bars on the windows, an illegal bike shop in an open garage, a rusted swing set,
a beaten-down white woman with stringy brown hair
pulling weeds from her lawn with dreams undoubtedly modest and difficult to attain. But these areas
were distinctly in the minority. For the most part, Simi
was all daylight, a place of clearly delineated boundaries, and I was aware, in driving around, of the neat-
ness and order of the city, the carefully thought-out

curves of its subdivision streets, its tidy and deliberate corners and curbs that seemed never to deteriorate in the climate, the Latino groundskeepers employed in its yards and gardens. The survey also reflected this broad concern with physical appearances, with the code enforcement of run-down or empty and abandoned houses, with street maintenance and repair, with sign ordinances that kept the place from looking "trashy and cluttered" like Los Angeles. There was even a desire to see a code enforcement hotline like the existing graffiti hotline, and not surprisingly, residents sought to minimize low-income housing. These were typical upper-middle-class suburban concerns, but with a heightened conformity specific to the valley, with its huge tracts of architecturally homogeneous housing and its overwhelmingly white and Republican population. Indeed, for the most part, visual order was a crucial component of the place.

This order was necessary not only for aesthetic and psychological reasons but also to maintain property values, but there were some who did not understand these imperatives. In particular, the valley's teenagers, more likely to dress unconventionally, listen to urban music, experiment with drugs, and in general to live in a kind of miasma of self-exploration, did not seem especially concerned with physical order outside the bodily. Moreover, teenagers, in their roving grasping at the world, might potentially cross paths with gangs, and these were deeply feared in Simi Valley, despite the fact that a police spokesman viewed the crime rate as "down in the last five years." Indeed, the citywide survey found Simi's residents "obsessed" with gangs. Some 30 percent of respondents described a terror of them, and although a highly unusual gang-related bike-by shooting around the time of the poll may have occasioned a heightened expression of it, it still seemed extraordinary. I had also seen it at the city council meeting, where there had been much mention of a disbanded gang task force that had recently been reconvened, high praise for the police department's "zero tolerance" for gangs, of the INS in gang sweeps that suggested the gangs' deeply foreign nature. When asked on the survey where any extra monies should be spent, people chose police and anti-gang activity by a wide margin, and two-thirds of respondents wanted more activities for teens, many mentioning the lack of teen activities as a primary cause of gangs. Even the sight of teenagers gathering together in groups out of doors aroused concern. "Every time they assemble as a group someone calls the cops and all the kids get chased off," was a frequent complaint, and teenagers spoke of feeling "encircled and stared at by the police department," particularly at the local malls or in parking lots where they liked to skateboard. A recent church-sponsored event that had attracted some two hundred teens had been going quite well until the cops came by to check things out, and then many of the kids had left in disgust.

The thirty or so students I spoke to at Simi Valley High confirmed the idea that the cops viewed them with suspicion. "They always park at those apartments right across from school to catch us doing something wrong," was a lament to which many assented. "A girl threw a cigarette out of her car and a cop gave her a $109 ticket and wanted her to pick up trash," recalled one girl; "you'll have three cops come by and give someone an $88 ticket for loitering." Another men-

tioned a stiff fine for jaywalking, and yet another remarked that when he was pulled over for what he was
told was a routine registration check, four extra officers showed up and his car was searched. The police
also seemed wary of the baggy jeans that young people have now affected from Connecticut to California,
and skateboarders complained about being told to
move on and having no place to skate. "They won't let
us go through the park," a thin, longhaired kid from
a group of six skaters I met outside city hall told me.
"They'll give you a $200 ticket and take away your
skateboard."

The teenagers knew, of course, that it wasn't just
the people dressing differently who took drugs or engaged in extralegal activity, but individual teenagers
of all kinds, whether trendies, jocks, gangsters, gang
wannabes, heavy metals, populars, computer nerds, or
any members of the group labels the young people dis-
liked yet used among themselves. Indeed, more than
half a dozen students described for me the huge parties
that could be found in Simi Valley nearly every weekend, thrown by an occasional twenty- or twenty-two-
year-old but usually by high school kids. Someone
would buy a keg or two of beer with fake ID, a flyer
would be passed around school with the time and location, and the host would charge a few dollars' ad-
mission. Since attendance at these affairs ranged from
seventy-five to even three or four hundred, they constituted quite a moneymaking enterprise for students
whose parents were away for the weekend, even if the
police did break them up at the 10 P.M. Simi curfew or
occasionally overreacted, like the time they responded
to beer-can-throwing Lemon Drive partygoers with
billy clubs. At these parties marijuana was often passed

around in bongs, and since the kids told me that there was "a lot of acid" around and that "shrooms"— hallucinogenic mushrooms—were "easy to get," undoubtedly these could sometimes be found at the parties, too. Indeed, such huge for-profit parties may have constituted something of a time-honored tradition in this state where the drinking age is twenty-one; my cousin Bill, who was providing me with the spare room in his condo, remembered the same kind of affairs from his own southern California high school days more than twenty years ago. "I've had between a hundred and fifty and two hundred people at my house, charging three dollars for girls and two for guys," a well-groomed and articulate young man from Simi Valley High told me, and when I said it seemed hard to believe he could have two hundred people over smoking and drinking without his parents suspecting a thing, he offered a trade secret. "I take 'before' Polaroids of each room and then I put everything back in its place. I tell people to smoke outside or in the garage, and I clean up every last butt until the place looks exactly the way it was."

When I thought about all this it began to seem as if the adult community saw itself and the world as a background brushed in with broad, easily comprehensible strokes. At a quick glance, if they saw nothing amiss, if their homes looked like the "before" Polaroid, they went about their business and assumed that all was well. But if something stopped the course of their glance and triggered an association with the disordered world outside the valley, there might arise an unease that would manifest itself in calling the police or dispatching a patrol car. That was why a young high school woman and her friends, driving around in painted faces and blue and gold clothes layered on or buttoned up backward, had been pulled over by the cops, and that was why, when they said they were coming from a football game, the officers instantly re-laxed: The kids had declared themselves part of the broad, familiar background of sports-related high jinks. Gathering youths who slouched about in baggy jeans, however, could not be so easily explained, and the well-groomed, articulate, visually All-American party host had implicitly understood this adult world-view and directed his demeanor and mop-up opera-tions accordingly. After all, if you came home and your house was in its usual order and your clean-cut, good-grade-receiving son seemed cheerful and relaxed, why on earth would you begin thinking he'd just picked up four or five hundred bucks selling access to fraudu-lently obtained beer and illegal substances?

There were, clearly, many things, including sexual-ity, that the teenagers voluntarily withheld from their parents, but there was a very real sense in which the parents were often not around. "A lot of times there's no one I can call—they all work," a youth worker told me. At least 60 percent of the students I spoke to went home to parentless houses in the afternoon, either be-cause both parents worked or because they came from single-parent households. Although almost half of all the kids had jobs, a necessity with prom tickets going for $135, plenty of them spent the after-school hours in front of the television or cared for younger siblings or made dinner for the family before their parents came home. Indeed, the commute to Simi Valley is somewhat longer than the L.A. area average, and though down from $260,000 in 1990 but still hefty for tract housing at $212,000 in 1995, the average Simi home price generally necessitates two incomes and so contributes to this domestic emptiness. "There are a lot of stressed-out parents, and there's a lot of denial," was the youth worker's view. "I see a lot of kids who graduate from high school who feel real empty inside, who have no mission in life or joy in living." "I don't really know my neighbors more than four doors down," a nine-year resident told me. "There's a lot of isolation." I heard suggestions of a higher-than-average domestic violence rate, heard Simi described by a social worker as "the incest capital of the world," and while these could not be substantiated, they were suggestions of trouble where it could not be seen, and these pieces of emotional information also seemed important because they were so rarely, yet so vehemently, expressed. If a high-ranking official at one school introduced me to the for-profit parties and the people who threw them, that person's counterpart at another school was full of how motivated the students were, how caring and involved their parents. If a mental health worker suggested I check into the suicide rates, the person I needed to speak to was usually away, and my telephone calls more often than not were unreturned. Simi seemed to desire no intrusion into its emotional life, which seemed subordinated to an image of order that kept the city forever focused on practical, if sometimes crude methods of preserving it.

With the exception of the main door near the administration office, for instance, all the entrances to Simi Valley High were chained and padlocked during the day, ostensibly to keep out gangs and drug pushers from the San Fernando Valley and Los Angeles. But the kids quite naturally felt locked in like prisoners, and while I was there, administrators were considering

the added step of bringing in police dogs to sniff out
drugs in students' lockers.

Curiously, my cousin Bill knew young people of the
very kind Simi Valley parents hoped their children
wouldn't meet. Formerly a professional musician, Bill
had taken a day job as an English teacher at Glendale
High School so that he could have a steady income,
and he had gravitated to the school's "alternative education" program through which some of the gangsters, as they were called, were completing their high
school educations. The alt-ed classes were taught in
trailer classrooms on the far end of the treeless, chain-
link-enclosed campus, and since his students were not
permitted to walk to the campus store without a pass,
Bill ran a food concession between periods at which
he sold burritos, Cokes, and other edibles at a small
but predictable profit. He spent the proceeds on
sound-mixing equipment for a music technology program he was initiating for which there was no other
funding. He had earlier offered a critique of American
high school administration while thumbing through
the Simi High calendar. "Every time there's a football
game, wrestling match, or volleyball tournament
it's in here," he sighed. "A rare band concert, but no
theater or art. And sports are all about winning and
crushing the opponent. It never once occurs to these
people that the arts are the one thing kids can excel in
where they don't have to compete with other people."
On the day I visited him at work, he was minding the
store.

"Did you get a look at his arms?" he whispered as
a muscular Asian kid in a T-shirt walked away un-
wrapping a burrito. "There are cigarette burns on the

insides of them—it's a gang initiation rite." I took a
stroll by the kid and saw them, round scars of dark-
ened flesh randomly dotted down either arm. Later
there was a fire drill and we filed out to the football
field, the heavily made up Latina girls in clingy and
low-cut black and the lanky, varicolored guys in
droopy jeans and homeboy caps. Bill introduced me
to one of the other teachers, a sensitive man in a
windbreaker who looked like an aging athletic coach.
"Some of these kids have been living on the streets
since they were eight or nine," the teacher said tiredly.
"Their parents left or did drugs or alcohol or beat
them. A lot of them have been struggling to survive
for so long that they don't have anything left. They're
emotionally stunted. They just can't feel anything."
Some of them found being burned an acceptable price
for being included in a human structure, and I could
understand the desire of the parents who'd moved out
to Simi to protect their children from such a lack of
self-love. Those parent's fears, however out of propor-
tion, were real fears. "The kids are scared at school
with guns and knives," a parent had complained on
the survey, and the week I was there an L.A. radio station carried an interview with a Simi Valley mother
who called the school system negligent for failing to
enforce its campuswide ban on weapons.

Still, the acquittal in Simi Valley of the four LAPD officers charged with the 1991 beating, kicking, eighty-six-
blow clubbing, and stungunning of motorist Rodney
King, who had been stopped in Los Angeles for speeding, seemed part of a time warp. The replaying on national television of an observer's video of the incident
had suddenly made available to all the undeniable evi-

dence of a type of brutal and long-private American occurrence. Millions of Americans and much of the world saw it and had an opinion, and the studied openness of King's treatment prompted nationwide investigations into police brutality and vigorous protests against the racism and barbarity of the Los Angeles Police Department. The trial of the four officers would normally have been held in the gritty downtown Criminal Courts Building in Los Angeles. But the defense sought a venue in less volatile territory, and the court went along, Judge Weisberg citing not so much the extensive publicity as the political turmoil in L.A. County. The trial, moved to more placid Ventura County, was held in the new East Simi Valley Courthouse, which had never before seen a criminal trial. Prosecutors had feared that Simi, home to many L.A. County police and fire officers, would produce a biased jury pool, but the jurors came from all over the county and only two actually lived in town. A number still had ties to law enforcement, however; one even had a brother who was a retired L.A. police sergeant, and most of them described police officers as polite and courteous people who had a tough job to do and tried to do it well.

The jury of seven men and five women, later six and six, reflected Ventura County. Ten of them were white, and for minority representation there was an Asian and a Hispanic. "I'm not surprised by the make-up of our jury," said defense attorney Michael Stone, who denied any defense plan to exclude blacks from the panel. "We did not consciously select or deselect any person because of age or race." But there had been only six blacks among the four hundred prospects summoned for jury duty. Against the odds two had

even made it into the jury box, but were later dismissed on the basis of their answers on question-
naires. And in many ways this was the meaning of
Ventura County. Unlike Los Angeles, it was rural
rather than urban, white rather than mixed, a land of
wide-open spaces and single-family homes a million
miles away from the world of Rodney King. And as the
trial moved on, even the photographs in the newspapers, of the experts, officers, and lawyers, were overwhelmingly white, the world of black and minority
Los Angeles largely undiscussed and unseen.

In Simi Valley city hall, across from the courthouse, many people were extremely surprised when
the acquittals came; they had seen the video like
everyone else. But soon, from over the hill and beyond the valley, word came that the verdicts would
be received with violence—and then the boiling
stew that was Los Angeles began burning. The city
planning office had to be evacuated twice because of
bomb threats, and Simi residents flooded the local gun
stores, bracing for hordes of angry Angelenos who
might march over the hills like an invading army seeking revenge. Rumors flew wildly—of threatened shootings and slayings, that the local police, beefed up
for the verdict, would be blocking off the Simi and
Moorpark freeways to check IDs before allowing cars
to enter the city, that a carload of young black urban
dwellers had been stopped at the Tapo Canyon Road.
*Mobile gangs*, and anger in south-central Los Angeles
took on the aspects of an uprising with battle lines
drawn, Simi a symbol of the opposing camp. From
San Francisco to Cincinnati and the East Coast and
back, protesters decried the city as bigoted, L.A. mayor
Tom Bradley reportedly called it racist, and Jesse

Jackson is said to have chimed in with "honky town."
Threatening phone calls came in, hate literature
arrived through the mail. There were, of course, residents outraged by the verdicts, people who were dis-
mayed by the lack of support around town for King.
"There are a lot of racists out here," one said, perhaps
implying that silence was a kind of collusion. Early
in the evening two women had gone to stand at the
intersection of Cochran and Sycamore, holding signs
calling for justice for King. That by 11 P.M. only seven-
teen people had joined them suggested both the
essentially private nature of the city and that people
were less than willing to come out against their community when it was under attack. However, "It just
goes to show how afraid people are to say anything,"
one protester was reported as saying.

"You have to feel some sense of responsibility for
it," Simi juror Chris Morgan said of the rioting that
left fifty people dead, and indeed, somehow, to the
country at large it no longer seemed morally possible
to dismiss the urban outrage, fueled yet rarely expressed during more than a decade of cut-back aid to
inner cities, as un-American. Even President Bush was
moved to call for federal civil rights charges to be filed
against the officers. He too had been forced to recog-
nize that the ideological structures that had once
made such verdicts unremarkable had cracked. The
middle-aged jurors had intuitively understood the
logic of battle lines and had bought the defense portrait of the officers as part of the "thin blue line" that
separated the lawless from the law-abiding. But the
protesting women and the eighteen-year-olds on
Simi's streets—and, indeed, millions of Americans—
had somehow felt connected to the world excluded

from the officers' trial; a great number of people
clearly found themselves on the other side of the law.

The verdict was only one in a series of events that
called upon Simi to question itself. Beginning in 1989,
the aerospace industries began laying off workers, re-
ducing to more of a simmer the once-blazing heat of
the southern California economy. There had been,
later, the closing of the GM plant in the San Fernando
Valley, further unsettling the economic structure on
which Simi and other subdivision communities had
been built. Periodic brushfires and the proximity of
the Topanga Canyon fires had also unnerved the valley. Finally, some twenty months after the L.A. riots,
the January 1994 earthquake had come. Since its epi-
center was in neighboring Northridge, Simi Valley was
hit hard. The rocking and rolling ravaged the Simi
Valley freeway and lifted the Boys and Girls Club
on Kadota Street off the ground. Many homes had
structural damage and had to be demolished; mobile
homes came off their foundations; roofs collapsed.
Hundreds of elderly people were displaced from the
city's five nursing homes; people had to stay in shel-
ters and stand in line to receive trucked-in water. Then
there were the aftershocks and their psychological tor-
ments in the ensuing weeks; enrollment in YMCA activities shot up because parents no longer wanted to
leave their kids home alone even for a few hours. Two
years later, the youth worker told me, some kids were
still trying to come to terms with the idea that the
whole physical world was built on a shaky foundation.

Given all this it is not surprising that Simi is concerned with being prepared for disaster and is the only
city in the county to have hired a full-time person to

coordinate emergency preparedness issues. I remembered a quotation from Ronald Reagan I saw on a wall in the presidential library, "We will always be prepared so that we may always be free," and while I was struck by the interrelatedness of the ideas of the conservative world picture, how neatly they all seemed to work together, it seemed that there was something a little easy, a little pat, a little superficial—in fact, a little tired and familiar—in the language I had been hearing all week. Simi remained tethered to a worldview in which conflict figured strongly. It was a community in which a police department representative told me he didn't see much difference between the man who had shot the graffiti taggers in the Zone and the Bernhard Goetz case in New York, in which Goetz, believing himself threatened, had shot four youths he took for muggers in a moving subway car. This man was certain that the Goetz case would never have been prosecuted in California. I was, he told me, an East Coast liberal—in a land of Reagan Republicans—to suggest that "we just can't have people discharging firearms in a crowded subway car"; and though perhaps it isn't easy, in the great openness of the West, to imagine the claustrophobic reality of a New York City subway car, it was clear to me that the third parties in the Goetz case, the innocent riders who had trampled each other getting away from an apparently insane gunman, simply were not a significant part of the equation for him. Indeed, the location seemed to him almost incidental to the conflict between civilized people and savages, order and chaos, good and evil.

The way of life the reporter had seen the people at the city council meeting defending also called for a civilized hero defending himself against savage

aggressors, and I came over time to see the guns and
the dogs in the high school and the submission to the
imperatives of preparedness and local authority as essential ingredients in a familiar drama. It was a time-
honored American story, resurrected by Reagan, and
Bush had finally presided over a crashing decline in
its relevance.

"Euro-American history begins with the self-
selection and abstraction of particular European communities from their metropolitan culture, and their
transplantation to a wilderness on the other side of
the ocean where conditions are generally more primitive than those at home," the cultural historian
Richard Slotkin has written in a three-volume study
of the influence of the frontier myth in American history. In time, these colonies created subcolonial settle-
ments farther into the wilderness. Thus American
colonial development "was linked from the beginning
to a historical narrative in which repeated cycles of
separation and regression were necessary preludes to
an improvement in life and fortunes." This narrative
was replayed daily in Simi Valley as its citizens went
"over the hill" and "outside the valley" to earn their
livings in the "primitive" and "gang-ridden" lands
of the San Fernando Valley and Los Angeles.

"Conflict was a central and peculiar feature of this
process," Slotkin continues; Europeans had to fight
the unknown wilderness and the nonwhite Indians to
whom it was home. Therefore, "violence is central to
both the historical development of the Frontier and its
mythic representations. The Anglo-American colonies
grew by displacing Amerindian societies and enslaving
Africans to advance the fortunes of White colonists.
As a result, the 'savage war' became a characteristic

episode of each phase of westward expansion." The "savage war" for many Simi residents was now the war on crime.

If the struggle against the Indians defined one aspect of the Euro-American identity, another key to it was the filial rupture between the colonies and England, and between the rough-hewn pioneers of the West and the Eastern centers of established capital. "The compleat 'American' of the Myth," according to Slotkin, "was one who had defeated and freed himself from both the 'savage' of the western wilderness and the metropolitan regime of authoritarian politics and class privilege." In addition to the savage war on crime, there was the conflict with the mother colony Washington, represented, for instance, by Feinstein, or by "East Coast liberals" or the "East Coast establishment"; and there was Ronald Reagan, the "traditional Man of the West," as his own museum called him, victorious in a "savage war" against communism and victorious too, against the metropolitan forces of big government giving aid to the inner cities.

The civilized man is a special kind of man who already knows about the inner workings of the savages, knows full well how deep a threat they represent. He is, of course, "the man who knows Indians," and part of his heroism stems from this knowledge and the use he makes of it. "The American must cross the border into Indian Country and experience a regression to a more primitive and natural condition of life so that the false values of the metropolis can be purged and a new, purified social contract enacted"; Slotkin goes on to describe a ritualistic "regeneration through violence" as if speaking directly about the man in the Zone:

> Because the border between savagery and civilization
> runs through their moral center, the Indian wars are,
> for these heroes, a spiritual or psychological struggle
> which they win by learning to discipline or suppress
> the savage or dark side of their own human nature.
> Thus they are mediators of a double kind who can
> teach civilized men how to defeat savagery on its na-
> tive grounds—the natural wilderness and the wilder-
> ness of the human soul.

Perhaps this was why, finally, the more emotional aspects of life, the loneliness and isolation, domestic
anger, sexual desire, or drug use, could not be quite
openly discussed. The forces creating such desires
were always there, of course, but rather than being
acknowledged, they were to be suppressed and controlled and tamed. The inner workings of emotion,
that space often referred to as the heart rather than
the head, are not, in the frontier myth, common human elements that unite both protagonists. One man
is fundamentally different from the other in his suppression of his inner forces. It is a world picture that
presupposes not the common humanity on both sides
but their differences.

American children have been playing cowboys and
Indians for many generations now, and indeed the
frontier myth has a long history. In 1893, when white
settlement of the vast undeveloped lands of the conti-
nental United States was largely completed and the
Indians effectively exterminated or controlled on
reservations, the historian Frederick Jackson Turner
offered a version of it so rhetorically compelling that
it provided the guiding force in American historiog-
raphy for more than half a century. But Turner's vision

of the transformation of the wilderness, first by the
trapper and the hunter, then by the pioneer and set-
tler, and finally by the agrarian farmer, as a series of
waves whose continual replication westward defined
the American experience and made it exceptional in
the world, was a product of nineteenth-century views
that championed the innate superiority of the "Anglo-
Saxon race." It conveniently excluded the experience
of Native Americans and blacks and Mexicans and
Chinese and all the others who make up the history
of this country, while exalting white men, the only
people then allowed to vote. Fortunately, historians
have been writing our more colorful past for some
years now, and the Western historian Patricia Nelson
Limerick believes that "inclusion has allowed historians to begin to offer a kind of society-wide psychiatric
service: just as an individual recovers from compul-
sion and expands the domain of choice with the help
of a psychotherapist, so a society can reduce compul-
sion and expand its powers of choice, with the self-
knowledge—sometimes painful
self-knowledge—gained through history."

By 1992 most Americans and even President Bush,
groomed for the job by the "traditional Man of the
West" himself, could see that the era of politics based
on an ideology of continual confrontation, whether
used to dominate Native Americans, the laboring
classes, African Americans, or the urban poor, was re-
ceding; even the global savage war of the capitalists
against the communists had ended. The frontier narrative has outlived whatever usefulness it had, and
perhaps the citizens of Simi Valley are already groping
toward a new narrative, because so many of them expressed, in the poll, the need for more cultural and

artistic activities in their city—those activities celebrating the complexities and creations of people rather than their stereotypes and destructiveness, those activities in which people can excel as individuals without being in contest with others.

This land is settled, and even if the least desirable portions have been left, most recently in the form of the inner cities, to those whose ancestors were physically and economically vanquished, it belongs to all kinds of people, and maybe someday that will be a basis on which to make a real case for American exceptionalism. But remaining at odds with each other is increasingly an anachronism. As more and more of the nation's wealth becomes concentrated in the hands of a smaller and smaller percentage of the population, more and more people have more and more in common economically. As America becomes more racially mixed, it becomes increasingly difficult to distinguish one kind of human being from another on the basis of color. The enemy is not so much abroad in the world as within ourselves, waging a savage war because it is too troublesome and difficult to change our habits of storytelling.

Would that the war were over, and peace at hand.

# Living on the Highway

In the early 1990s, the aptly named Mall of America, "en-closed, encyclopedic, endured," as one writer saw it, epito-mized the ever vaster scale of real estate projects in the United States. Developers sought permits for hundred-acre or more parcels of land and created subdivisions bigger than entire towns used to be. Cities and towns no longer ex-panded by single, idiosyncratic buildings but by hundreds of houses or tens of thousands of square feet of retail space; massive blocks of construction arose, their forms dictated by corporate chains or a developer's latest economic triumph; the landscape testified to an undeniable hegemony of big capital.

In isolated moments, landing at a new low-slung airport on green level land, say, and driving a rental car onto the interstate, America seemed a pleasant and forward-looking nation, a quiet place of separated spheres with blue skies and breathing room for all. But soon enough there were the jan-gling and ubiquitous hard-edged vistas of metal and concrete and the endlessly replicating franchise chains; since city cen-ters were increasingly run-down, by 1984 more than half the nation's office space was located in the burgeoning suburbs. The only way to get around in these white-collar worlds was to drive. "The [American] road is now like television, violent and tawdry," James Howard Kunstler declared in The Geography of Nowhere in 1993. Its landscape

> is littered with commercial buildings and commercial mes-
> sages. . . . We whiz by them at fifty-five miles an hour and
> forget them. . . . We did not savor the approach and we were
> not rewarded upon reaching the destination, and it will be the

same next time, and every time. There is little sense of having arrived anywhere, because everyplace looks like noplace in particular.

Colorado looked like Ohio looked like New Jersey or Florida or California in a blunt and standardized statement of corporate power, and the majority of Americans now lived within these chaotic landscapes dedicated to sales, turning away from the past in older cities.

(And why was this? What was so collectively hard to face? The country's settlement under a racist ideology of Manifest Destiny, the enslavement of blacks and ethnic cleansing of the Indians, dressed so gaudily in the rhetoric of freedom?)

Strip had changed the meaning of the word urban in America. Interstate growth was now the norm in some of the nation's fastest-growing metropolitan areas, many of which—Seattle, Portland, Salt Lake City, Denver, Las Vegas, and Phoenix—were in the West. Indeed, 86 percent of all Westerners now lived in cities. Four-fifths of Utah's population lived along an eighty-mile strip near Salt Lake City; in Colorado a 110-mile drive of subdivisions and megastores connected Fort Collins and Denver and Colorado Springs, with Pueblo and Boulder close by; in Phoenix, fifty miles of development flanked both sides of the Superstition Freeway. Attracting some fifty thousand people a year with jobs in computer technology, telecommunications, and other high-tech fields, these cities had grown with help from the savings and loan boondoggle. But they had also encouraged sprawl, partly through a tradition of cheap, abundant land, low taxes, and minimal government interference— "Nobody in this town has ever said no to a developer," a Phoenix anti-sprawl activist has been quoted as saying—but also by going on road-building sprees. "We're going to build roads, and lots of them," Utah governor Michael O. Leavitt was still proclaiming as late as 1995, although his state and others *were billions short of the money needed just to maintain them.*

*Highways were a sure-fire, subsidized way to attract development. Between federal highway funds and the tax base that businesses brought, cities growing this way were flooded with cash in the short term. In the long term, of course, sprawl made everybody's day longer, worsened the American dependence on cars and oil, and brought documented health hazards from auto emissions. Since the mid-1950s, the number of vehicle miles driven in the United States increased three times faster than the population. In some cities the situation was even worse. Seattle, whose development proceeded along enormously expensive Interstate 90, quadrupled its vehicle miles traveled between 1980 and 1990 and ranked fifth nationwide in traffic congestion. California was also up there; Phoenix, on 469 square miles of land and as large as Delaware, was physically larger than Los Angeles with only a third of its population. The issue went further than hassle and health and environmental hazards; it also came back to whether the development governments were subsidizing was a quality product. "We spend tax dollars to encourage sprawl, and then it comes back to us as air pollution," one Phoenix resident summed it up. The days when the Arizona desert was a great sanitarium for sufferers of emphysema, tuberculosis, bronchitis, and asthma were over. By the mid-1990s, according to the EPA, the air in Phoenix was among the dirtiest in the nation after Las Vegas, New York, and the mother of all car cities, Los Angeles; from outside Denver, an observer could watch how "the afternoon sun . . . mutate[s] the brown cloud into a great purple smear that obscures the city, like an inland sea."*

*It did not have to be like this. Europe has drawn boundaries around its cities for centuries to centralize development, and in the early 1970s, Oregon, a pocket of common sense in the Northwest, passed a law that called for its cities to write land-use plans to limit sprawl. The law was controversial, but referenda held to strike it down in 1976, 1978, and 1982 never succeeded because the will of the Oregon people was against sprawl. Portland officials drew a line around the city in an effort to push jobs, homes, and stores into a smaller metropolitan area surrounded by a greenbelt of trees and farmland. The city dismantled a downtown freeway, created a well-attended riverfront park, and added a light-rail system that has exceeded expectations in its popularity. Moroever, the city has managed to attract five hundred thousand people in the last decade and a half. Indeed, many of the corporations who came, including Hyundai, Hewlett-Packard, and Intel, claim that they did so because they liked the idea of having fruit orchards and streams so near to town, and home prices in the area have risen nicely.*

*Other cities are beginning to follow Portland's example. In 1994, Seattle, beginning to see development in the Cascade foothills, enacted an urban growth plan that even downzoned an area that was to include new homes into a rural and forest area. And although it turned down mass transit for freeways in the 1960s, it has just voted to have a mass transit system; smaller California cities like San Jose have also created boundaries, and residents of Missoula, Montana, have voted to spend millions to buy open land to keep a greenbelt around the town.*

*But such strategies don't always work, as the forces of sprawling development are often far stronger than its foes. In Colorado, even the animals are trying to let people know that they are overstepping their territory. There have been cougar attacks and cougar and bear sightings exceeding a hundred a year when they were rare ten years ago; elk spilling into suburbia from Rocky Mountain National Park have to be tranquilized to remove the tomato cages, wind chimes,*

clotheslines, and electrical cords that get caught on their
antlers. "People are moving into animal habitat," a wildlife
researcher states simply. And yet in sprawling Denver, a
Phillip Morris subsidiary is building a subdivision that will
accommodate ninety thousand people. In statewide meetings where residents are asked what they want the state to be
like in fifty years, Colorado's governor Romer is trying, as
he says, "to motivate people community by community to
mold their own destinies" rather than let developers do it for
them. Boulder, too, has tried to oppose development at the
local level, at first buying up greenbelt land with a sales tax
back in the 1960s and then setting a 2 percent cap on residential growth in the 1970s. But the director of parks and
open space for Boulder County, which has bought up forty
thousand acres in the years since 1975, knows that they're
not really making progress: Colorado loses ninety thousand
acres of rural land a year to subdivisions and malls. And
Denver, only thirty miles away, creeps closer.

## Please Play the Machines While You Wait

"Vegas? That's the last place I'd ever want to go," said a New York friend who knew only the stereotype. And the night flight really was like an upscale bus to Atlantic City, a retired crowd playing cards and drinking before a touchdown dash to the neon-sheathed casinos on the desert floor. Slot machines and metal palm trees in the airport. And my sister Allison, waiting in her new Ford Escort at the curb. "Not bad, eh?" she said proudly, switching on the air-conditioning for the midnight drive to her apartment complex. She lives in the other Las Vegas, the nation's fastest growing city of the past decade and a boomtown to make a developer's heart beat faster, and before she moved here for the big job there was no car at all and a furnished apartment with mismatched wallpaper. But all that's in the past. Within two days of arriving, she had a cool, pastel apartment at the Palm Cove, a loan from the credit union, and was out shopping for a new car. She had landed, after all, in the latest Sun Belt scene of the American dream.

"A lot of people with bad credit come here to start over," the president of her credit union had said.

Las Vegas reminded me of southern California, a city of bright mornings and distant mountains, of palm trees and cars and billboards along open patches of roadside. Like a small, clean, still-in-control Los Angeles, it feels prosperous and new, with good roads and new firehouses and subdivision homes with the

red-tiled roofs and pale stucco of California mission
architecture. Apartment complexes with names like
Catalina Shores, Crystal Cove, and Martinique Bay
suggest a glimmering coast a few miles away, all calling out to youth and health: COME LIVE WITH US!
HOT TUBS, SAUNA, STEAMROOM, GYM. In typical
Western fashion, housing has been built out rather
than up: From the freeway, low-lying skyscapes spread
to the horizon; ribbons of strip commercial cut lanes
around the subdivisions. In the distance, a familiar
brown haze hangs, not yet over the city, but against
the horizon line of red rock mountains. Well over 90
percent of all households have cars, and they give the
place the unsettling feel of a specially sought out but
as yet unpolluted territory.

Las Vegas blooms with the plastic primary colors
of the giant chains. No used book or furniture stores
or family immigrant restaurants in sight here, but
7-Elevens and Pizza Huts and Carl Jr.'s and Texaco stations and the rest of the unvarying familiar architecture of the corporate bottom line that one city planner
called "natural growth." Along the sun-baked strips
are the great supermarkets, of housewares, furniture,
groceries: The Phar-Mor than-is-necessary store, where
the seven-foot-tall shampoo and conditioner rack is
175 feet long, and shopping is a distended, almost un-
derwater experience: The clerk down the aisle is too far
away to call out to. And back in the car, I found that
classical music contradicted the great rolling reel of
late-twentieth-century developer landscape continually
unfolding before the windshield. It was too old and
European, too rooted in centuries when nothing had
happened here; only bland commercial rock seemed
in tune with the plastic gas stations and the sleek new

lines of the developments. "I can *only* listen to classical here," Allison said in surprise when I mentioned it,
"as a kind of counterbalance to all this." And in a day
or so I too was using symphonies to offset the mental
impact of the roads. They're the same ones found all
across America, only in Vegas there's the newer variation: The strip commercial is punctuated by city blocks
of six-foot-high adobe walls, keeping the noise, exhaust, and commercial life from the residential areas.

Allison's clean, modern apartment at the Palm
Cove was indeed a pleasant haven from all that. Each
evening as I walked in a bathing suit and T-shirt past
the two-story neomission units to the serenely landscaped pool and saw the stars and the moon and
the airplanes loaded with marks coming to land at
McCarran Airport, I felt, as I was supposed to feel, safe
and rich. The complex had been built far enough from
the road so you did not hear it; there were no sirens or
radios; speed bumps and circles slowed the incoming
cars. Even at 8 A.M., when people might have been going off to work, I rarely ran into anyone, even at the
pool. It was always quiet, the doors forever shut
against the silence.

"We should go see the cactus garden, it's right
across the street from my house," Allison said, turning
through the complex gates at the end of a day when
the hum of the car ran through my head like a fugue.
"Sure," I said. "We could take a stroll over; I like the
idea of getting out of the car." "Well, it's kind of a long
walk in the heat," she said, and of course she was
right. *Across the street* has no meaning in Las Vegas,
where going anywhere requires moving from space to
space shut off from the outside, from one climate-
controlled location to another. The almost constant

lack of fresh air, the slamming of the car door, the click-off and -on of the radio or television or air conditioner or ceiling fan: One afternoon when I pulled into the complex and stepped into the silent heat, I realized I was not in a city at all: It felt absolutely nothing like urban life.

Horses multiplied too quickly in the New World to keep ownership a privilege. Pickup races along quarter-mile paths, cock fights, boxing bouts, and shooting matches were common diversions early on in the country's settlement, but the landed gentry in Virginia, importers of racing stock who aped the aristocratic gambling of the British, wanted restraint. Public gaming moved west, to the old Southwest along the Mississippi River. Ornate New Orleans saloons sent faro, craps, and three-card monte to rowdy under-the-hill fleecing dens in Natchez and Vicksburg and Louisville, where the loners and get-rich-quickers who had already staked or lost everything to be there liked the fast-paced optimism of betting. Gambling flourished; so did professional dealers, known as blacklegs. Relying on cheating rather than percentage and volume, they earned a criminal reputation that fluctuated wildly with the social climate, although respectable citizens often held sizable interests in local gaming halls. By the 1830s, as Native Americans were forced out of their Southern lands, plantation life moved west. Precariously maintaining slavery by a rigid, class-stratified social code, the plantation elite hated the unconventional gamblers, who, loath to turn away paying customers, saw no harm in dealing to blacks or the poor. Even the election of Andrew Jackson, who speculated extensively in land, killed a man and nearly

himself over a debt, and saw in gambling the enterprising individualism of the West, had not helped to
forestall the inevitable. Convinced that dealers had
backed a nearby slave rebellion, in 1835 local justice in
Vicksburg hung five blacklegs, declared martial law,
and sent gamblers packing as town after town along
the river followed suit.

The gamblers had two choices: the Mississippi itself
or the trail to the Gold Rush, and they soon embraced
both. Between 1840 and 1860 floating river palaces
had tables piled with gold dust; well-dressed riverboat
gamblers, ready cash handy in their rings and chains
and watches, took on the legend of folk heroes who,
according to the current bigotries, specialized in bilk-
ing foreigners, Jews, and the wealthy. But all the elbow
room was in the West; and in the "pandemonium of a
city" that was midcentury San Francisco, European
travelers were shocked at the number and opulence of
the casinos. Inside the famed El Dorado, bright chandeliers lit up huge paintings of voluptuous nudes
while the orchestra played all night. Most gold diggers
lived in crowded boardinghouses or canvas tents, so
the warm gambling halls, with their food, drink, and
daily newspapers, were logical places to spend the
evening, their luxurious settings nightly rekindling
the hope of instant wealth.

But soon San Francisco's railroad stretched back to
East Coast culture like an umbilical cord, and with
respectable theaters and restaurants came the lynch
mob. Gambling went underground. Californians
nonetheless were soon hopelessly speculating on commodities, railroads, diamonds, and real estate, and
nothing could match the mining stock ventures that
came with the discovery of the Comstock lode in west-

ern Nevada. In the mining towns gambling halls were reappearing overnight, and outside the stock trading offices on California and Montgomery Streets in San Francisco, feverish crowds clamored for the latest prices. "Your washerwoman had ten feet in the Highflier," remembered Bret Harte. "Your office-boy held certificates for 50 shares of 'Aladdin.' Everybody talked stock."

No sooner had the mines slumped than Los Angeles boomed, the speculation this time in property and oil. Between 1880 and 1930, fortune-seeking immigrants quadrupled the population. The housing market, the auto trade, the movies—there were so many ways to make it that people just kept on coming. Los Angeles had never felt a real attachment to the East, and the city's suburbanized way of life suggested a new breed of American metropolis—but the pattern of gambling remained the same. Promoters sold L.A. as a clean-living community with a mavelous climate, and gambling was relegated to the clandestine clutches of organized crime. By 1931, when depression-starved Nevada relegalized gambling, Californians could breathe a sigh of relief at having open gambling outside its borders and yet so close to home.

A frontier town of wooden sidewalks and whiskey saloons when the Los Angeles-Salt Lake City railroad made it a switching point in 1905, Las Vegas depended on the growth of Los Angeles. Faltering when the mines closed in the 1910s, it found new life when the L.A. highway was paved, and in 1931, the construction of Hoover Dam, built to supply southern California and the West with abundant water and power, flooded the newly legal Fremont Street casinos with payroll cash. By the 1940s, to gawk at the dam and gamble,

tourists were arriving by car and train in the casino al-
ley nicknamed "Glitter Gulch," a street flanked on one
end by air-conditioned auto courts and on the other
by houses where "women sat around," as Erle Stanley
Gardner described them, "—waiting."

Few could have predicted the once-in-a-century
forces poised to make Las Vegas a great gaming capital.
Almost every decent-sized city had had illegal gambling outside its city limits, and with the establishment economy revived after the war, the usual
campaign to eradicate it arose—just as troopships full
of men who had learned how to gamble in the army
arrived home. Somebody had figured out how to air-
condition large spaces, and all the black market
money floating around after the war had to be in-
vested *some*where. "Multitudes of men were ready to
lose their shirts in cool desert casinos owned by professionals with criminal connections sponsored by
dirty money," one observer summed it up, "and
Nevada said OK." Soon it was impossible to park in
Glitter Gulch, and casino-resorts like El Rancho Vegas
and the Last Frontier spilled out to the Los Angeles
highway. Fremont Street clung to its Old West image,
but the new "roadtown" known as the Strip was pure
L.A., predicated on the car and descended from the
Miracle Mile. When Bugsy Siegel built his tropical
pink-and-orange Flamingo casino-resort, the town was
liberated from its tired western tune and stepped directly into fantasy. Glitter Gulch, a gambler's Times
Square of old-time popcorn lights and shaded sidewalks that has now been enclosed mall-style, continued to do well. But it was only on the Strip that Las
Vegas attained its lunar-landscape megareality, its

atom-blasted technicolor, its climate-controlled satis-
faction, and its worldwide wild reputation. The scale,
the color, the movie star divorces—all the glamour and
imagination came straight from Hollywood. The frontier theme was a nice idea, but Las Vegas was strictly a
twentieth-century town.

There are slots in the bus stations, bars, video stores,
pharmacies, groceries, liquor stores, and even Kmart,
haphazardly scattered little moneymakers, but they
are only reminders of the casino districts passing
for downtown in Las Vegas. In the early 1990s on
Fremont Street, there were still topless dancers, and
the storefront gambling joints made no pretense at elegance: "In just twenty minutes . . . pick up your FREE
computerized gambling horoscope," read the card
proffered outside a chintzy little slot machine hall.
"Please play the machines while you wait." On the
Strip, where zooming property values forced up high-
rises, the evening desert cool brought on cosmopolitan sidewalks, hectic and crowded and bright and loud
with neon and honking traffic and a spitting-fire vol-
cano fountain; inside the casinos, magicians, can-can
girls, and all-male revues, drinks and bare shoulders
and Monte Carlo chandeliers, handsome men of all
races strolling the floor in thigh-revealing togas.
Polynesian huts, rain forests, Venetian streets and pirate ships, animal acts and trapeze artists, window
dressing all for the gambling trade, a twenty-four-hour
circus that slows down, in the day, with the heat of
the sun. Then, for the locals who don't want to lose so
much they can't come back tomorrow, some tables
lower their bets to two dollars. It's a world fueled by

intermittent alcohol and cheap protein fixes, the 99¢
bacon and eggs special, the $1.99 strip steaks, the 75¢
canned shrimp cocktail topped off with a blob of red
sauce: food to keep going, food to keep betting, food
to keep you right in your own little gambling world.
Games of chance are a sport for only one, where each
alone will beat the palatial house and rise above the
masses to be rich. Husbands and wives welded into
indifference can finally be alone before the slot machines, can shut out the unbearable everyday. Gambling can't be understood by observation; and to watch
it in Las Vegas is only to glimpse its mind-boggling
extent. There are so many huge casinos with people in
them, hundreds in one and the next and the next and
the next, hundreds and thousands in front of the
slots, the tables, even placing offtrack bets, thin bat-
tered compulsives with cigarette-smoked faces, their
sickness at losing so familiar it seems normal; the curiously plentiful, harmoniously married seniors with
their gambling money neatly budgeted; good-looking
middle-aged women whose painted fingernails wrap
around the cool wet of cocktail glasses; even gamblers
in wheelchairs: relaxed to sensuality in their leisure,
solemnly attentive in their greed, believers all in a re-
ceding dream. I wandered from casino to casino
watching them and finally felt numbed, thinking of
the owners upstairs laughing their heads off, and I
leaned back against any old Roman column at all, lis-
tening to the endlessly jaunty ding and clang of the
slot machines, and closed my eyes like Nelson Algren,
"sick of seeing them come in begging to be hustled,
wondering where in the world they all came from and
how in the world they all earned it and what in the
world they told their wives and what, especially, they

told themselves and why in the world they always,
always, always, always came back for more."

Mob control eventually gave way to corporations like
the Hilton, Holiday, and Ramada chains, and today
Las Vegas stands in the face of the entire history of
American gambling, because no matter how settled
and respectable the rest of the town becomes, it will
never be able to outlaw gaming. Nor would it want to.
A conflict between the gamblers and the upright folk
is really unthinkable, since they've reached a mutually
advantageous legal accommodation. The casinos are
allowed to make obscene amounts of money, and
their businesslike owners drop enough steady cash
into Nevada's coffers—some 40 percent of the state's
revenues—so there's no state income tax; and every
new hotel room adds jobs to the economy. And yet
the industry generates only a dubious product or service. Basically exploiting the irrational, it holds out
the lure of wealth without working and is linked to
the medically recognized addiction of compulsive
gambling, which affects some four million Americans
and their families. Gambling has been so controversial
for so long that Las Vegans have obviously had to
make a psychological adjustment to it, and most of
the residents I spoke to tried to insulate themselves
from the casinos.

"You don't have to have anything to do with the
Strip if you don't want to," half a dozen people must
have volunteered without being asked, and when
Allison first arrived, she was advised to live on the east
side of town so she could live and work without ever
having to cross it. Historian of gambling John Findlay
has noticed how, over the years, Las Vegans have tried

to mentally remake the city by downplaying the importance of gaming. In the 1950s, they tried to miti-
gate their decadent image by patriotically embracing
atomic testing; in the 1960s, a convention center
helped residents believe the city had more than one
career. Las Vegans have also chosen a residential life
that protects families from the Strip, all, as Findlay
put it, "responses to an uncomfortable environment,
reactions that, like maintaining well-watered lawns
in the middle of the desert, seemed to make the
metropolis more acceptable" by making it more like
other American communities. For apart from the casinos, Las Vegans live a kind of irreproachable life:
Consumers of new cars and new construction and the
brand-new commodities that keep the economy moving, they are virtuous participants in American life
no different from more than half of Americans, who,
according to the 1990 census, now live in similar suburban enclaves. Still, the need to minimize the impact
of the gaming industry was something I heard over
and over.

In fact, like a kind of American fantasy ritual, denial is a consistent theme in Las Vegas. There is the denial of the bleakness of the desert itself, accomplished
by sleights of hand of which indoor living is only one.
There are the residential complexes named and designed to suggest waterside vacation resorts: "At one
point almost all the housing developers were putting
in a waterfall or a fountain—and we just can't allow
the use of water that way," complained a county official. There is the bright green grass of these complexes,
watered during the night from sprinklers built right
into the turf, a practice long encouraged by low water
prices. There are the artificial lakes—a private one

spans some thirty acres—in a city whose growth will
be limited more than anything else by water, the lakes
finally banned by Clark County as completely inappropriate. But pressure from hotels and builders ended
an early 1990s moratorium on excess water usage, and
Las Vegas went back to allowing unrestricted growth
and began looking for distant water supplies.

There is the denial, in a metropolitan area of some
900,000 people, that public transportation is truly
necessary. There was the discovery that the bus connection I needed off the Strip came only every hour
and fifteen minutes; there was the schedule confirming that the majority of buses run once an hour. Only
down the Strip, a profit-making route for the private
company running the bus system, did they come
every fifteen minutes. Voters, mostly in cars, haven't
been especially forthcoming about subsidizing routes,
but even beyond that, the city's spread-out zoning
precludes the population density needed to make
mass transit work. Las Vegans are stuck with the car
as a way of life, and to be without one, I discovered
as I walked to my appointment, is to walk long blocks
alone under a hot sun breathing car exhaust; it is to
be excluded, stranded, cut off from the pace of the
city.

There is the apparent lack of concern that the smog
blighting Los Angeles, Denver, and even Phoenix,
cities so many people came to Las Vegas to escape,
might have the same effect here, a denial seen in the
sprawling urban design and heard in the voice of a Las
Vegas sociologist who dismissed the unmistakable
brown smear I saw each morning by saying that the
Indians had long ago noted a haze in the valley. At the
bottom of it all is an unconscious denial that pollution

is a serious issue—although the city's carbon monox-
ide levels have been ranked with New York's
as the fifth worst in the country. Local government,
which lured the private bus company, financed a
downtown transportation depot, and has lobbied for
carpooling, a fleet of new buses, and increased fuel ef-
ficiency, knows there is a problem but must contend
not only with voters and outdated, lax air pollution
standards but also with the powerful casino lobby,
which, unwilling to tolerate three months of mid-Strip
construction, brought down plans for a clean, magnet-
ically levitated people mover to connect downtown,
Strip, and airport—an innovation that would have
been the first of its kind in the United States.

All booming cities face delays in the development
of infrastructure, but the interests of Las Vegas residents and the casinos and developers are often at
odds, a dilemma not helped by the stubborn belief of
many of Clark County's elected officials that the free
market will solve all problems on its own. Clark
County has long been unwilling to interfere with business growth. It could, for instance, exert pressure on
developers to create affordable housing, but doesn't
really want to, although at least thirty thousand
people need it. "This is an example of a city that is extremely progrowth, where the market has proceeded
without impediments, but where we still have homelessness, we still have crime, we still have drugs and all
the other urban problems anyway," a planning official
told me. The police are known for brutality and loy-
alty to the casinos; street gangs and drive-by shootings
are continuing problems. Las Vegas has been known
as "Mississippi West" because of its historically rigid
color line, and after the Rodney King verdict, a man

was pulled from his car and beaten and another died
in flames when violence erupted on the city's west
side, the other side of the old railroad tracks, that is
not, somehow, a place for hotels, banks, supermarkets,
or even regular bus service. After the violence the casinos reportedly agreed to hire three blacks each in visi-
ble floor jobs in a gesture to the Las Vegas where
there's been no boom at all.

Many of the thousands of new Las Vegans, however,
come from cities that have already been destroyed
in the American mode, and as voters they have, albeit
after the fact, become concerned about the carte
blanche that has been handed to business. By the
early 1990s, almost every community in Clark County
had asked for a plan to compel incoming businesses to
comply with community goals, and this turn to government to oversee development was a welcome
change to Las Vegas planners, who would naturally
like to avoid the mistakes made in other cities and
keep the place livable. A forward-looking species, the
planners I met chose not to dwell on the dismal past
but always to look ahead to the future.

"Why don't you take a drive out to Summerlin?"
one of them suggested.

As I entered Summerlin from poor and barren Lake
Mead Boulevard, lined with billboards for the usual
water-themed subdivisions, the commercial edge disappeared. At Sun City Summerlin, the newest Del
Webb luxury retirement community, I asked a guard at
the gate for directions and he sent me down a wide,
palm-lined drive. A couple of miles down, a series of
discreet signs led to an attractive little building housing the Information Center. There seemed no need to

lock the car. Inside, a cheerful, well-dressed sales representative welcomed me. "Would you like to watch our video?" she suggested, leading me to the plush sofas of the video viewing area. Struck by how well-off so much of the United States is, I pressed the sofa-side control panel. And then the music, the cheerful, soothing voice of the advertising man: ". . . Summerlin . . . twenty-two thousand pristine acres . . . acquired by Howard Hughes . . . named after his grandmother . . . perched high above the glittering lights of Las Vegas . . . close but far enough away . . ." Advised to visit Summerlin by a representative of the City of Las Vegas, I was unprepared for the new town's outright denial of an urban identity: "Summerlin . . . everything suburban living was meant to be."

Planned to house some two hundred thousand people, Summerlin is really just an enormous network of subdivision homes starting in the low $100,000s. The development was packaged by Hughes's Summa Corporation, which approached the city with a plan that would allow a municipal investment in roads and sewers to be recouped with property taxes. The differences separating it from ordinary developments are obvious: It has been planned not just as a complex but as a town, though one largely predicated on the car. More than four thousand acres have been set aside as open space; extensive bicycle and pedestrian paths weave through the community; a park system offers tennis and other amenities. Retail developments have been placed near, but not too near, the houses. Churches, office parks, a medical facility, a library, a performing arts center, and private and public schools complete the idea of a place where one can "live, work, and play." In its embrace of the natural environment,

in its emphasis on preservation against both development and crime, Summerlin represented, in the early
1990s, a new strain in the American suburb—one that
has seen communities in Houston and Phoenix and
Los Angeles lose their investment value with too much
strip commercial and overdevelopment. Summerlin
is corporately planned living—with input from the
City—that permits escape not only from urban crime
but from the big-business casinos and corporately
driven commercial strips.

Landscaped to encourage water conservation, the
houses of Summerlin, beautifully constructed with expensive tiled roofs and other high-quality details and
amenities, are surely, as the video narrator claimed,
examples of some of the finest new construction available on a mass scale; but they are also monuments to
protection and control, to the loss of the pedestrian
world, to the privatization of American life—a privatization fashioned out of the fear of others and the consistent need to control the personal environment.
Even the preference for shopping in the privately controlled mall rather than a public Main Street expresses
a desire to avoid the unpredictability associated with
public urban life. And this inwardly turned, munici-
pally sanctioned community will, it would seem,
succeed in segregating itself from the poor. For
Summerlin, likely to house employees of the high-
tech computer and military aerospace firms lured from
California by the so-called South Nevada Industrial
Revolution, is open only to income levels clearly
those of management, articulated as if there were no
other types of people in the world. "A range of distinc-
tive homes for every lifestyle . . . from entry level to
executive . . . from custom golf course home sites and

gated communities to retirement neighborhoods . . .
Summerlin is a place where it's possible to move
up . . . without ever moving out!"

On a less grandiose scale, this was what the Simi
Valley had been like almost thirty years ago. As I drove
away, past the golf course hosting a national tournament that reminded me of Hilton Head, past the enormous construction projects spread out for miles
through a landscape even more silent than that
around Dallas, I thought about how the people in
Summerlin would never have to witness the great social horrors of American inner-city life. It seemed to
me then that the bleak vision of architects Andres
Duany and Elizabeth Plater-Zyberk referred not simply
to the design of suburbs but to the whole machine of
American development:

> The classic suburb is less a community than an agglom-
> eration of houses, shops, and offices connected to one
> another by cars, not by the fabric of human life. . . . The
> structure of the suburb tends to confine people to their
> houses and cars; it discourages strolling, walking, min-
> gling with neighbors. The suburb is the last word in pri-
> vatization, perhaps even its lethal consummation, and
> it spells the end of authentic civic life.

Allison's orange cat Mango had not enjoyed the move
to Las Vegas. At first he hid in out-of-the-way spots in
the apartment, but had gradually ventured out onto
the shaded patio. He had only been taking the air for
a couple of days, however, when a violent desert storm
came up suddenly. The lightning and crashing were
more than the creature's frayed nerves could stand,
and, in a moment of the most self-destructive tor-
ment, he ran away.

The poor brute. Every Palm Cove unit looked exactly the same, with the same outdoor electrical units, the same doors, the same line of cars, the same strip of grass outside, and the same landscaping shrubs; I could imagine his confusion in trying to figure out which was his home. But the structure of the complex made it difficult for us to find him. I should have realized this the afternoon we were heading out to the pool and I grabbed a FORWARD TO WORKER POWER T-shirt out of my sister's closet. "Please don't wear that," she asked me earnestly; she was trying to make friends there, and who was I to pass judgment? Hadn't I refrained from wearing an abortion rights shirt because I had neighbors who were pro-life? And I knew what she meant because I too sensed that at the Palm Cove we were in a rigid, intolerant environment. There were just too many rules. Residents could not dry clothing on their patios—this energy-efficient use of the desert sun might denote the lower classes. One could not perform car repair in the parking lots. There was the rule against lawn furniture, radios, and non-regulation plantings. Other complexes had other rules: A homeowner in a new subdivision told me he could paint his house one of only four colors; a friend staying overnight had to pull his Winnebago into a special parking area. These residential restrictions are worked into leases and deeds: You can tolerate your neighbors because they have legally pledged themselves not to be different.

These rules led to difficulties in finding Mango. Hours spent walking the grounds calling him had proved fruitless, and a campaign involving the neighbors was clearly in order. Flyers, however, could not be posted on trees or lampposts, and door-to-door solicitation *of any kind* was expressly forbidden. The only

place to post a notice legally was in the main lounge
of the office, but in so large a complex it was hardly
enough. Even there, the complex manager, Donna,
had watched Allison closely, checking the size of the
flyer and the way it was affixed. "I thought you had a
tabby named Lulu," Donna said. "Mango's just visit-
ing," Allison countered—the companionship of a cat
costs an extra twenty dollars a month, and she felt
that paying for one was more than adequate. "This is
absurd," I said. "Xerox some flyers at work and we'll
stick them on some windshields." But in the end we
had to sneak them on the cars because this too was
forbidden by the lease. The rules inhibited people
from interacting even to help an innocent animal
wandering the desert, but you could hardly be angry.
It had all been agreed to beforehand.

Over twenty-five years ago in *Fear and Loathing in Las
Vegas*, Hunter S. Thompson saw the hideous heart of
the American dream at Circus Circus casino at two in
the morning, but over the years the trapeze acts and
the Ronald McDonald stupidity of its huge roadside
clown have come to seem harmlessly nostalgic. For
me the real horror was at the southern end of the Strip
at two in the afternoon, inside the fake stone walls
of the Excalibur casino hotel. Through Excalibur's
Disneyesque forest of huge white castle towers, escala-
tors ascend through a moat-guarded bridge; thunder,
trumpets, an imposing voice of welcome and behold:
a slate-floored entrance hall from which I could
see long lines of families, many of them Mexican
Americans, waiting at the hotel registration desk. On
the basement level there were carnival games, Robin
Hood bows and arrows, pop-gun shoots for pink

stuffed dogs, and *kids*, running around as if this place had nothing to do with a casino; the smell of fried hamburgers was never to dissipate in Excalibur's four fabulous levels of fun. In a way it was like driving along the commercial strips, trapped in a vision of man-made materials and mass-produced food, a mass consumer culture on a scale so grand and epic most people seem to take it for granted.

The 4,032-room Excalibur, whose reasonable week-day night rates in the early 1990s kept occupancy near 100 percent during the high season, was the first major resort aimed at lower-middle-class families, and it was the prototype for the new, family-style Las Vegas. The town once focused on the high rollers—the $80,000 a year executives who came to PGA tournaments and dropped a few grand at the tables. But no longer. At some $290 million, Excalibur was far cheaper to construct than the high-roller haven of the Mirage at $615 million. And where the Mirage needs to take in roughly $1 million a day to break even, Excalibur needs far less. Casino owners have been quick to copy the concept. The Luxor, an Egyptian-themed resort, is marked by a huge glass pyramid hotel, Nile rides, a ten-story Sphinx, and 2,526 low-priced rooms. Nearby is the MGM Grand, a 5,009-room casino-hotel and theme park touting a yellow-brick road and Emerald City concept. Mirage owner Steve Wynn has opened an "adventure resort" called Treasure Island that boasts battles royal, pirate ships, and cannon blasts. Disney executives have reportedly flown over these desert lands in search of properties, and of course there is New York, New York.

Just as the casinos of the 1950s caught the atomic technological wave in their futuristic decor, and the

crystal chandeliers and fabulous interiors of the 1980s
gambling halls reflected the exalted expectations of
the Reagan era, so the new casino-theme parks appeal
to the lowered expectations of Americans in the
1990s. Attracting more people to take cheaper vaca-
tions, the casinos hope to make up in volume the
profit that fewer people used to provide. With the decline in educational standards of the broad American
masses, there are more and more people who will take
places like Treasure Island and the MGM Grand to be
good theater, just as many people who patronize
Disney World mistakenly take it seriously as a funnel
for history and culture. At a cost of some $2 billion,
the theme-park casinos represent a tremendous investment in what Marc Cooper has called "an increasingly
adolescent national culture," which apparently enjoys
being awestruck by mechanical dinosaurs before heading home to the suburbs to which they have fled from
scary cities; to believe, as the country generates low-
paying, nonunionized service jobs with no health
care, that we can still afford the luxury of fantasy.

But whether marketed as sin or theme-park entertainment, casinos have been favored by mobsters and
corporate heads because they generate never-ending
rivers of cash. As journalist David Johnston put it in
*Temples of Chance*, "A hotel with a casino can net more
money *each week* than a plain hotel of similar size
might net in a year or even two." Especially after the
Reagan decade, states and municipalities have been
grateful for a piece of this pie. In the 1980s, when
wealth flowed out of the public sector and into the
private, ordinary Americans spent much more money
on gambling, trying to beat a house where the national odds have only become steeper. That this essen-

tially morally empty activity, now clothed in Wizard of Oz gear, should experience such a tremendous boom seems eerily manipulative, and that it is embraced with such unquestioning insouciance is sad and poignant and even tragic.

But Las Vegas seems to feel pretty good about the money and the new squeaky-clean image the theme-park casinos are bringing to town. And with one of the best entrepreneurial climates in the nation and one of the lowest corporate tax rates, Las Vegas is set to boom for a while. Because the desert provided a tabula rasa for untamed capitalist interests, the city is one of the best places to see the corporate influence on American life, from shopping to transportation to housing to entertainment, to see how business interests have created a number of separated, enclosed worlds where there are no common goals that cut across class lines. In all likelihood, Las Vegas will continue to sprawl outward into the vast desert lands classified by the Bureau of Land Management as "disposable," the latest example of the American penchant to leave the places where the dream has died for unspoiled territory in which to begin again.

A week after Mango's disappearance, Allison spotted him on one of her searching walks in the silent afternoon; puddles from the night sprinklers had undoubtedly kept him alive. Life kept going on, and I got on a plane heading east.

# Déjà Vu

The kind of development I'd seen in Las Vegas was going on elsewhere in the intermountain west. In the six years ending in 1991, the New York Times reported in 1996, some two million people had moved into Oregon, Washington, Arizona, Nevada, Utah, Idaho, and Montana. More of them were from California than anywhere else, middle-class baby boomers vaguely searching for a small-town America they had never really experienced, and they didn't care that their new states had low per capita incomes because they did not plan on working for $6.50 an hour. Fleeing traffic, pollution, crime, and a state increasingly saturated with poor immigrants, they took the capital built up in their well-paying jobs and high-priced California homes and bought reasonable homes or businesses in places where the air was clean and the population almost pure Caucasian. It was white flight at the state level.

Originally, Los Angeles may well have been a new kind of city in layout and transportation, but in its decline its middle-class citizens acted as they had in many other places. Like the whites who fled older inner cities in the 1960s and 1970s following urban riots, like the manufacturing concerns that left Stamford and other unionized Northern cities for the unorganized white, rural labor force of the South, so too Californians with capital have engaged in a uniquely American cycle. I often wondered whether it would ever end or whether we were to keep knowingly repeating it again and again, the new cities becoming economic and social disasters like the abandoned ones.

Certainly, Phoenix had always hoped it would not

167

*become another Los Angeles, although it did little to fore-
stall that fate. Indeed, it was as if all these cities were pre-
tending that dirty and decaying Los Angeles, with its
disparity between rich and poor, had never happened. "We
are repeating the mistakes of L.A.," the former mayor of the
Denver suburb of Castle Rock has remarked, "but it's hap-
pening slowly, so that the average Joe only sees part of it, like
the traffic congestion, and doesn't connect it to everything
else."*

The periodic movements to new territory were testa-
ments to optimism, surely, and to a can-do spirit, but there
was also within them a tremendous sense of entitlement.
Geography, after all, could be overcome: Complexes were
built atop landfill, and fake lakes were scooped and carved
from the earth. As with highway funds and the savings and
loan money, states and cities looked to the U.S. government
for water. Some four billion federal dollars have been used
to bring water from the Colorado River into Phoenix and
Tucson, although at least Arizona demanded proof of adequate water prior to development. Nevada had no such re-
quirements. Las Vegas *"promises water to virtually all new
developments—regardless of the prospect of shortages,"* the
New York Times *noted, and the city was now looking to
distant sources for water, as Los Angeles had done at the
turn of the century. Some suburbs in still-expanding Denver
were built without secure water supplies and live always
with a fear of scarcity.*

And sometimes the antigovernment attitudes of
Westerners inhibited community facilities. Utah, for instance, put a cap on what municipalities could charge developers for roads and sewers and also decreed that when
property values rose, the overall tax rate had to fall, so that
the better an area's homes, the worse off its schools will get.

*In like manner, Denver limits the percentage a school district can get through property taxes, so that its population influx cannot adequately help its schools. "New but malnourished schools, subsidized sprawl, tax structures that ultimately bankrupt growing communities—these problems were never part of the master plan of the new Western cities," the* New York Times *declared, but I doubted whether there had ever really been a master plan. The city planning offices in Stamford, Las Vegas, and Dallas had lacked the economic resources to say no when developers presented demands, for with so many funds cut in the Reagan years, they could not afford to let tax bases go to more pliant localities.*

*This lack of foresight and the habit of thinking only about oneself and family, this unwillingness to invest in community enterprise, this desire to remain in one's own house and to keep one's own expenses low all seem strangely similar to the way cities and towns hoped the government would pick up the tab for water and roads. It's all about passing the cost on to someone else; the idea, over and over, is to minimize one's responsibility to the community. The large-scale failure of Americans to envision themselves as part of a history-making process seems extraordinary; and it would seem that there is as great a resistance to planning for the future as there is to living with the past.*

*The need to start over on unspoiled land, so profitable to the individual developer, is ecologically wasteful and historically ignorant. Former Albuquerque mayor David Rusk, who has studied the patterns of more than three hundred cities, has found that there is a fundamental correlation between the rate of sprawl and that of flight. Detroit, for example, which has lost a million or so people, consumed land at thirteen times its population growth. "My rule of thumb," he*

169

*says in a sad omen for the West, "is that the faster the rate of sprawl, the faster the rate of abandonment." How depressing to see the American earth treated as something disposable, to be used up and thrown away, the ultimate expression of a consumer society.*

# Celebration:
# A New Kind of American Town

In late 1995, shortly after Disney announced the $19 billion takeover of Capital Cities/ABC that gave it television access to 99 percent of American homes, the entertainment giant opened the preview center for Celebration, the residential town being constructed on its vast Orlando acreage. The project had been launched in the all-around bad year before. Disney Paris, very publicly losing millions, had had to be saved by $400 million from a Saudi prince; co-chief Frank Wells died, and hit-movie wizard Jeffrey Katzenberg jumped ship; Michael Eisner, his remarkable decade of success winding down, needed quadruple bypass surgery. Perhaps most galling, in 1993, when Disney had proposed a theme park near a Civil War battlefield in Virginia, a hive of stinging intellectuals had served up resounding indictments of Disney history and the crass commercialism spawned by the parks in Florida and California. The company ended up looking like a big bad business ready to plunder the sites and content of American history and had to pull out.

In such a climate, the $2 billion Celebration venture was a logical business move, particularly after Disney World's successful resort hotels and the timeshare Vacation Club the company launched in the early 1990s. Disney Development Company president Peter Rummell has also said that he hopes Celebration will alter Disney's image as a purely entertainment

conglomerate, and Eisner has stated many times that
he wants to use Celebration as a showcase. Indeed,
Celebration is more than an ambitious attempt at re-
viving classical town-planning principles. It is a high-
profile advertisement for what business can provide
that government cannot, and both it and the Capital
Cities/ABC merger raise important issues for American
democratic and civic values.

In 1964, when Walt Disney quietly amassed some
27,500 acres of central Florida swampland bordered
by sugar plantations and a sleepy little town called
Kissimmee, the forty-three square miles of water and
green seemed the perfect antidote to what he called
the "distracting and conflicting elements" that had
grown up around the cramped 160 acres of California's
Disneyland. Today, the reality immediately outside
the Walt Disney World Resort, the world of U.S. Route
192 in Kissimmee—whose name in the Indian language Caloosa ironically means "Heaven's Place"—is
a noxious example of unchecked chain-driven strip
development, with no discernible regional culture.
Palms and an occasional strip of golf-course grass
are the only tokens suggesting either Florida or the
un-mass-manufactured world. Minizoos, fun houses,
themed dinner shows, McDonald's, Shellworlds, and
Texaco stars merge primary-colored plastic and neon
with metal, asphalt, and signs that blink and rotate in
computer digital. The strip has the look of something
completely unplanned, something distant corporate
oil, motel, and restaurant chains just extended and
extended through the great expendable American
landscape. "It's ugly, it's awful, it's appalling," an
*Orlando Sentinel* columnist has described the strip

growth since Disney. "You live here every day as a
Floridian with a tremendous sense of loss."

By the late 1980s U.S. Route 192 had become a liability even to Disney. For one thing, the lower-end
clientele that stayed at the strip motels and patronized
the thriving black market in resold Disney tickets
spent too much money outside the Disney compound;
the company preferred people like its EPCOT visitors,
mostly professionals with a median income of some
thirty-five thousand dollars a year. Then too, strip
commercial, now ubiquitous across the nation, was increasingly associated with the lower classes. So in the
1980s, Disney began building themed resorts on its
property so that its guests would never have to go outside. Because the Florida legislature's 1969 dispensa-
tion gave the company unprecedented power to build
whatever it wants, county officials watched helplessly
as more than ten thousand new rooms were constructed on the property, knowing they would mean
the marginalization of smaller businesses on the strip.
This kind of private flight from commercialization will
undoubtedly continue to occur all across the United
States. Because of its impoverishment, the public sector has been unable to effectively restrain corporations
and developers who build along outlying lands around
cities and freeway interchanges. In so doing it has
failed to protect all Americans from strip dreck and the
high turnover of minimum-wage service workers in
chain franchises who, in an earlier era, might have
been providing personalized service as small stable
businesspeople. So it is ironic that Celebration ex-
cludes both visual corporate commercial hegemony
and government that has failed to secure those very
"cornerstones" of Celebration—education, health,

technology, place, and community—that Disney is marketing in the town.

Directly off 192, a deeply calming drive lined with the white rail fences of horse country leads into Celebration. There is no security gate; you simply drive past the greenbelt golf course and right on in. Like American small towns before World War II, Celebration has tree-lined streets and houses with front porches; parks, a school, and a downtown shopping district are all within walking distance. The homes, linked to the school and businesses by a fiber-optic network, are a blend of traditional American styles; and there are townhouses and apartments, as well as a golf course, swimming pool, tennis courts, and a health care center devoted to wellness. The idea of Celebration alone was so popular that, at its first offering, three times as many buyers came as there were lots to be sold, and Disney had to devise a lottery to accommodate them.

Inside the home sales headquarters, 1960s home-movie clips with a saccharine voice-over feature images of bake sales, spaghetti dinners, and kids on bicycles followed by dogs, but Celebration's downtown is decidedly sophisticated. Planned by Robert A. M. Stern and Jaquelin Robertson, it is oriented around Market Street, a short, brick-paved stretch lined with dignified palms, bordered on one end by a placid artificial lake and on the other by a landscaped seating plaza complete with water fountain. A café, clothes boutique, restaurant, grocery, and other shops, none of them chains because this is a *home*town, line the street. Taking cues from older Southern cities like Charleston and Savannah, Market Street has old-fashioned street

lamps, a clock tower, and sidewalks shaded by the balconies of apartments above. Passageways lead off to
little side gardens or fountains, and the bright orange
and pastel buildings look clean and splendid in the
Florida sun.

Past the plaza Market becomes Water Street, its traffic lanes flanking a man-made creek crossed by pleasant little bridges. Water for the golf courses, parks, and
lawns is pumped up from the lake through a tunnel
and then flows through this creek back into the lake;
Water Street itself leads out into the residential areas.
There are town homes, cottage homes, village homes,
and estate homes in Celebration, in ascending price
and degree of luxury. The town homes are closer to
the downtown, but the single-family homes, grouped
for the most part by price range, are spread throughout the development. Residents can choose Victorian,
Coastal, Classical, or Colonial Revival, with a smaller
number of French and Mediterranean styles. Most
neighborhoods have a park nearby. On Veranda Place,
cottage homes cozily surround a little green highly
reminiscent of Savannah, and on a lovely August day
people were outside enjoying their porches and eager
to talk. The nearness of the houses to the street made
me feel easy and included, and I was surprised at how
intensely familiar it all felt. The houses have been organized in a way that is deeply American down to the
traditional mailboxes on the curb, and I had forgotten
that architecture could feel this good.

The new public school, under construction and op-
erating in its first year out of the Teaching Academy, is
planned as a low, Mediterranean building, and on parcels outside the surrounding golf course, Celebration
also has an office park of tall and attractive Italian-

inspired buildings; for the most part these house the
Disney Development Company, however, and only
by chance will town residents work there. The health
center under construction may also be used by residents depending on their medical coverage.

Of the 350 homes to be built in phase one, about a
quarter are estate homes, starting at around $425,000;
120-odd are village homes, priced between $200,000
and $315,000, and sixty or so are cottage homes,
which cost between $150,000 and $200,000. The
reasonable-sounding one-bedroom apartments starting at $600 a month and town houses starting at
$127,000 make up a relatively small part of Cele-
bration; large-scale master-planned community construction makes the most profit on the higher-priced
homes. And just as the Disney Vacation Club encouraged more stable, repeat consumption than the theme-
park resorts, so Celebration has created a more stable,
permanently fee-paying population.

Still, its literature and employees suggest that
Celebration is less a business venture than the fulfill-
ment of Walt Disney's original dream for EPCOT. Although mostly perpetuating Disney as a charismatic
leader with a mission the entire Disney machine feels
proud to follow, the idea is not completely far fetched.
"EPCOT will be an experimental city," Walt Disney
said in a text endlessly quoted by biographers and
critics,

> that would incorporate the best ideas of industry, gov-
> ernment, and academia worldwide, a city that caters to
> the people as a service function. It will be a planned,
> controlled community, a showcase for American
> industry and research, schools, cultural, and educa-
> tional opportunities. In EPCOT there will be no slums

because we won't let them develop. There will be no
landowners and therefore *no voting control*. People will
rent houses instead of buying them, and at modest
rentals. There will be no retirees; everyone must be employed. [My italics]

In Celebration, these last two elements of Walt's
vision clearly had to be axed, because selling homes
makes the venture profitable and because people later
along in life are clearly more likely to be able to afford
the properties.

"When Walt pointed to a map of Central Florida almost thirty years ago," Eisner has declared, "he described a community where he would like to raise his
family. We looked at what had made communities
great in our past, added what we've learned from the
best practices today, and combined this with vision and
hope for strong communities in the future." Actually,
however, in spite of important differences, Celebration
owes its largest debt, designwise, to the New Urbanism,
an architectural movement spearheaded by Andres
Duany and Elizabeth Plater-Zyberk, designers of the
Florida Seaside resorts and the Kentlands development
in Maryland. The movement's mission has been to urge
builders to create suburban developments on the scale
of small towns, increasing their density and putting
shops, schools, and recreational facilities within walking distance of the homes, gearing plans toward pedestrian and public transportation, humanizing and
enlivening streets with balconies, stoops, and porches,
and placing garages in alleyways behind houses whenever possible. Having arisen with no ties to Disney,
New Urbanism is a response to tract housing and strip
commercial sprawl, a revolt by architects against the

energy-wasteful and identical mass subdivisions of earlier decades. Celebration's main architects, Stern and Robertson, are advocates of this school, but Celebration differs from New Urbanist principles in fundamental ways. Unlike other architects and planners, Duany and Plater-Zyberk write an overall code that controls both buildings and other parts of the plan, so that other architects may design individual buildings without violating the spirit of the whole. This allows variety and idiosyncrasy within an coherent overall whole, as at Seaside. By contrast, Celebration has no code; instead, it has the enforced variety of Victorian, Colonial, and other styles of houses, each of which must be a set number of units away from its next repetition. Disney rigidly controls Celebration's looks. Duany and Plater-Zyberk's codes avoid legal language and are written in plain English. They also presuppose a community of trustworthy and committed residents, and Celebration most emphatically does not presuppose this, although Disney has gone to great lengths to suggest that it does. Celebration is a community-interest development (CID) governed by the autocratic rules that usually govern CIDs. And it is in the overall context of increasing numbers of CIDs and private control that Disney's promotion of Celebration as a traditional American town, evoking a mantle of equality and democratic representation, deserves exploration.

Disney has gone to some trouble to present Celebration as a "real" town. Like any publicly governed municipality, Celebration has its own post office; the public can drive or walk right into the town. The golf course is public on a daily fee basis, the school is owned by the Osceola County School District, and Osceola also provides fire and police protection. But Celebration is not a town in the way the term has been traditionally understood in the United States. In the American town Disney purports to emulate, all the sidewalks, parks, recreational facilities, and public places belong to the public domain, or government; here, all of these, along with the infrastructure, belong to Disney.

Indeed, Celebration may be the first "town" that is more private than public. Within it, however, the boundaries between these realms are invisible, as aside from the absence of gates, numerous clues suggest a public town. An American flag flies from a pole on a downtown green; the dark, rough-hewn sign in front of the Celebration pool is the kind typically seen at a state park entrance. The Disney-owned parks and sidewalks look like parks and sidewalks anywhere; and officers from the Osceola County sheriff's office ride the streets in patrol cars. But the pool is for Celebration residents and their guests only, and the officer I spoke to at midmorning was there off-duty at Celebration's request, earning $16.50 an hour, a bonded, highly trained employee to supplement Disney's security, which patrols less conspicuously at night. Finally, there is the town hall. Designed by Philip Johnson, made of dark red brick and surrounded on all sides by cheap-looking square metal columns, it is centrally located and almost universally disliked, the unease it provokes undoubtedly more than architectural: There is no town government as Americans know it.

All these sights suggest far more civic authority than there actually is. But then, rather cynically, Disney has a twenty-five-year history of unobtrusive control. Its security has always been a highly guarded secret, and for Disney World employees, there is "on-stage," where the public can see, and "backstage," a world of tunnels, elevators, cafeterias, and other work sites, where it cannot. According to the authors of a Disney study called *Inside the Mouse*, for employees to be on the Disney acreage is to be "on property," and, incredibly, nobody ever dies at Disney World—even the man at EPCOT who shot himself in the head and sent his brains flying was kept alive by artificial means until he was "off property." Also without its visitors' knowledge, Disney hires "shoppers"—some might call them spies—to make sure its workers keep up their good Disney cheer at all times. The company avoids bad publicity by having employees agree when they are hired to "waive their right to discuss in print particulars of their job"; those who leave unwillingly must sign a "witness statement" detailing the circumstances of their departure. Meanwhile, Disney's labor system is highly compartmentalized, one room gathering one kind of data and another room another, while someone further up decides what to do. "This is a world," one contributor sums it up, "in which all social planning has been replaced—as every attraction at EPCOT's future world predicts and hopes it will be—by corporate planning, every advance in social coordination conforming to and confirming the logic of the company's needs."

Aside from its houses and lots, Celebration, too, is a Disney-owned world, and as a CID, it will likely foster that nonparticipatory CID culture that will aid Disney's need to control. One resident remarked that although there were no gates, he felt confident Disney would put them up if they became necessary; many

residents I spoke to said they were investing in
Disney's security and integrity. And at the same time it
generates this confidence, Disney also suggests that it
can provide better planning and security than government can. "Much of the unique infrastructure sought
by Celebration was either unavailable through normal
government channels, or simply too expensive for
local government," explains an article in Disney's
*Celebration Chronicle* describing why the roads, fire
protection, water systems, and other pieces of infrastructure are so impressive. Government, as we all
know, is increasingly abdicating its social role. We can
still count on it to pay for wars, of course, and for
costly bailouts of large corporations and the messes of
high-flying savings and loan thieves. But these large
expenditures, alongside huge tax cuts, have made
government too poor to finance decent education
or architecturally planned towns. Government is a
second-class estate, and simply not as rich or as powerful or as able to make things happen as Disney.

Then why a public school in Celebration? Well, for
one thing, the idea of safe public schools, often helping to sell real estate, is another piece of nostalgia, and
one embedded in that prewar era Disney so wishes to
emulate. Robert A. M. Stern told me that Disney
wanted a public school because a private one would
have "seemed too elitist," and this seems consistent
with Disney's constant worry about its image. The
Osceola County School District was already in the
business of running schools, and using existing organizations and people makes sense. But Celebration
School is not your ordinary public school, and not
simply because it is a brand-new facility, wants to
mandate school uniforms, subscribes to a humane-

sounding personal learning program for each child,
and puts a pleasing emphasis on the arts. All to the
good, it will have substantial input from residents,
who will be more likely to participate in the school
than parents who live far from where their kids are
bussed to school or who work long hours at low-
paying jobs. But Celebration's schools are unlikely
to be racially diverse. Disney advertised with racially
inclusive images and in the minority media, but
Celebration has appealed primarily to whites, probably because it evokes nostalgia for a time when the descendants of Western Europeans defined middle-class
life and blacks, Jews, Asians, and other ethnic minori-
ties were systematically excluded from suburbia; the
town's idealization of this heritage has little appeal to
those whose parents were poor or unassimilated or excluded from it. Florida schools, by contrast, are ranked
among the lowest in the nation, ill-equipped, over-
crowded, and swamped with immigrant children with
deficient English skills. These children, however, will
make up at most 20 percent of the "public" school in
Celebration, for the arrangement is that 80 percent
of the students will come from Celebration itself.
Moreover, unlike most Florida schools, the one in
Celebration will have help from the Celebration
Company, the Disney affiliate behind the town. The
school, owned and operated by the Osceola County
School District, will be managed *with input from* a
three-member board representing the Osceola County
School Board, Stetson University, and the Celebration
Company. Moreover, the Teaching Academy adjacent
to the school, owned outright by the Celebration
Company, will also have input, and is backed by be-
tween five and nine million Disney dollars and grants

from other sources. Its main goal, a fact sheet explains, will be to "serve as the on-site professional development center for teachers at Celebration School as well as educators throughout Osceola County, Florida, and the nation." That the professional development center for a public school should be owned by the Celebration Company is, to put it mildly, a unique approach; but this is a school where a language arts teacher told me about the "WALT Works" program she was using and where a framed, full-length photograph of a dashing Walt Disney in baggy pants hung on the wall as if no one had the slightest thought that shilling for Disney in a public school was not only unnecessary but completely inappropriate. Indeed, Disney stands behind the Celebration School in the way once-wealthy government used to stand behind the traditional public school. And this avuncular position is crucial, not only because it helps Disney retain control, but also because it provides something else that the government used to provide, and that is moral authority.

That Disney manages to emerge from the Celebration venture with its moral authority intact and even heightened is a central point because moral authority legitimates power. Celebration is a world in which the balance of power Americans have long been used to has radically shifted. It is a world in which government has been subordinated to business, is an adjunct to it, and not the other way around.

Given Disney's nationwide real estate projects in New York, South Carolina, and elsewhere, its immense media power, its growing retail outlets, and its continuing inroads into publishing, the arts, the media, and culture generally, it may be useful to review the company's ideological history.

According to most accounts, Walt Disney's father was a Eugene Debs supporter and an unlucky businessman who tended toward bitterness and beat his sons. Young Walt found escape from the old man's dour nature in an early love of movies and animals, and at eighteen he began working as a cartoonist in Kansas City. He moved to Hollywood in his early twenties, started his own studio, and began to have success with a cartoon creation he called Mickey Mouse. After 1929, however, managing a business without much capital became extremely stressful, and in 1930 Disney had a breakdown brought on by the strains of trying to stay afloat in a sea of economic collapse and rising animation costs. By the late 1930s the studio began to profit from animated features like *Snow White*, *Fantasia*, and *Pinocchio*, but instead of rewarding his employees, now numbering more than a thousand, Disney plowed his earnings into a new studio building in Burbank, only to see his profits drop with World War II. In 1941 his employees went on strike, and, refusing to consider that the problem might be one of management, Disney saw his employees' betrayal as the work of communists; mediators were able to settle the dispute only when he left the United States for a goodwill tour of South America. The strike set Disney on a politically rightward course, and his feelings for his employees seem never to have been the same.

Significant for American culture, however, Disney promulgated the idea that entertainment and storytelling could be detached from politics and social issues, much as he sought to separate his own creative

instincts from his life with his father. This detachment
and its partner, a surface patriotic gloss, were grate-
fully accepted during the Cold War era when voices in
American literature and film that criticized society
were being systematically stifled. But this excision of
social conscience trivialized the moral potential of
Disney's work, and because he saw social content as
unnecessary and perhaps even un-American, he
gained no expertise in exploring people whose cus-
toms and cultures were different from his own. The
result, over the decades, is that much of what has been
created by the Disney company has depended on
stereotypes. Disney's 1946 cartoon feature *Song of the
South*, for example, depicted so benign a relation between Southern master and slave that the NAACP
protested vigorously; in 1971 the Chilean writer Ariel
Dorfman and the Belgian sociologist Armand
Mattelart analyzed Disney's skewed portrayals of the
First and Third Worlds in *How to Read Donald Duck:
Imperialist Ideology in the Disney Comic*, a classic of children's literary criticism that has been translated into
thirteen languages. As late as 1992, administrators at
Disneyland only suddenly discovered, after the Los
Angeles riots, the many nice young people with black
and brown skins who could be hired to work there.
And the Disney World that I reviewed in 1992 was
awash in simplistic and dismaying representations of
foreign cultures. The Magic Kingdom's Jungle Cruise,
for example, passed a group of "Pygmies," as the pilot
called them, surrounded by shrunken heads—although the Pygmies are forest, not river, people, and
they do not shrink heads. The imperialist vision in
EPCOT's Mexican pavilion was also offensive. Pas-
sengers in little boats bobbed along an underground

"River of Time" past scenarios in which half-naked figures, like someone's hastily conjured-up idea of native
savages, danced to indistinguishable commentary. A
tourist come-on film showed bikinied gringas sipping
pineapple drinks in a pool; a pottery exhibit had a
woman shrieking: "Pleeeese, señor, won't you buy?"
and a balding man calling "Sale today!" further added
to the impression that Mexican sales pitches come
from an ethnic identity instead of grinding poverty.
"I am surprised at the low level of education among
people in such a rich country," a college-age Mexican
worker at an outdoor cantina told me in Spanish.
"They are so healthy, so nicely dressed. Yet some have
asked me, Do you have television in your country? Do
you have cars or do you get around on mules? Many
cannot tell if the birds in those trees are alive or mechanical." Casually, he asked if I knew that the huge
pyramid housing the Mexican exhibit was a fake: He
could never be sure how seriously Americans took
Disney representations.

At moments like these it is easy to see the harm
Disney imparts to our culture and to see, too, why so
many intellectuals dislike the company and worked so
vigorously to thwart its plans for a history theme park
in Virginia. While Disney has consistently sought to
*simplify* experience and avoid complexity as if it were
a frightening disease, serious artists and intellectuals
devote their lives to expressing the *complexity* of experience, to helping people see that life has no easy answers, that issues affecting people must be carefully
thought out, that there are differences in our ways of
living that must be understood if we are all to live
together. It is in this sense that Disney really is,
as Robert Stone has remarked, "an evil empire."

Let the buyer beware.

Many people believe that business is more cost effective than government, forgetting that business works toward a profit margin that government does not need to collect. Moreover, private enterprise discriminates on the basis of class. Corporations are deeply hierarchical structures rather than egalitarian ones, as the recent exposure of the pension protection corporate executives claimed for themselves and not their underlings makes clear. That lower-class people are excluded from Celebration was to be expected—it is a private town. Yet just as it must once have seemed impossible to imagine that the religiously segregated neighborhoods and country clubs in my home county of Westchester, New York, might one day seem other than obvious or natural, or that one day racial segregation might strike much of the nation as odious, the concept of social segregation by class, which has a history as stultifying and horrible as that of race or gender, may also one day appear odious; after all, academics have been looking through lenses of "race, class, and gender" to counterbalance the overkill of white male scholarship for quite a while now. Unfortunately, the increasingly less powerful government has generally been the means of redress of such grievances.

Finally, private enterprises are not accountable, even in theory. Unlike governments, they don't have to supply information about themselves; as Marc Weiner has noted in the *Nation* on books killed by publishers, the culture industries in particular like to keep their activities secret. When I began gathering information, I wrote to the Celebration Company and received news mailings from them for many months;

when I called to discuss a visit, however, a public relations representative informed me that because I was working on a book project, the company could not provide me with information on their "American town." This was, she explained, because of Disney's "synergy with Hyperion Press," a New York publishing house. That by this logic their "synergy" with Capital Cities/ABC would preclude their talking to any newspaper, magazine, or broadcast journalist did not seem to have occurred to them. Nor, apparently, did it bother them that this policy is most restrictive to people doing serious, in-depth work. The British professor of social research Alan Bryman, author of *Disney and His Worlds*, was also rebuffed by Disney, and other writers have suffered the same fate. An inquirer is either someone Disney wants to cultivate for business reasons or does not; professional courtesy is not a factor, and even lower-ranking Disney employees make striking examples of how instantly superfrosty otherwise normal people can become, as a chance encounter in the Celebration office park parking lot reminded me. Perhaps this is a skill refined in the "Disney University."

What Disney has shown of itself in Celebration is homespun, traditional, small scale, innocuous, and easy to imagine, an utter abolition of the corporate grandiosity of the 1980s. But in truth Disney is global, high tech, megascale, secretive, and ruthless; its power and reach are hard to fathom. And while disdaining the franchise chains in Celebration, Disney's own stores replicate endlessly in the malls. Moreover, Celebration architects, residents of Celebration, and a Hyperion author I met at a party all extol the vastness of wealth that Disney brings to their projects, but not

all this wealth is decently gained. Recent reports from
the National Labor Committee, a nonprofit workers'
rights group funded by religious organizations, foundations, and twenty-three unions including AFSCME,
reveal that Haitian workers making Pocahontas
T-shirts and Lion King children's outfits make only
about thirty cents an hour, leaving them malnourished and living in squalor. Sometimes "only five
cents for every $11.99 Disney garment they sew," says
Charles Kernaghen, who visited factories in Haiti and
showed the Haitian workers a Disney shirt he had
purchased in the United States at a Wal-Mart. "When
I translated the $10.97 into the local currency —
178.26 gourdes . . . all at once, in unison, the workers
screamed their shock, disbelief, anger[:] . . . the sales
price of just *one* shirt in the U.S. amounted to nearly
five days of their wages." In late 1996, Disney was
still declining to meet with Haitian workers to discuss
a wage increase; it is also interesting to compare their
wages with the $96,700 *an hour* that Michael Eisner
earns. Disney also subcontracts to factories in Thailand,
where child labor is used, and in Myanmar, formerly
Burma, where workers also receive pennies an hour.
But the company will not have to abide by UN sanc-
tions forbidding new American corporate investment
in Myanmar, however, because it is already well established. Seeking now to penetrate the as yet untapped
Chinese market, for which even more Disney toys and
pajamas are likely to be needed, Disney increasingly
dreams of foreign deals. When Eisner came on board,
overseas business accounted for only 9 percent of the
company's intake; in recent years those revenues have
approached 25 percent. Given Disney's public relations
know-how, it is highly unlikely that Americans will

hear about these stories in any depth on ABC affiliates, but they can remind us of the earlier global shipping economy of 1600–1800, which was dominated by slave-produced commodi-ties made in countries too distant to bother the consciences of their consumers.

With the Capital Cities/ABC acquisition, at the time the second largest merger in American history, Disney became in one blow the mightiest entertainment company on earth. It also gained the resources with which to create and shape a great deal of American opinion, far more than it has already exercised by presenting racist stereotypes to hundreds of millions of unsuspecting vacationers; the ABC television network, after all, is the one most Americans turn to for news. That the largest news network in a country long known as the capital of the free world should be owned by a company that doesn't believe in freedom of expression for its workers is irony enough. That it should also have built its own town, dispensed with traditional American government, installed itself as the state, and sold it all as an improvement is ominous testimony to how easily we continue to be seduced by hype.

# The New Urbanism

Disney's need for control aside, I was sufficiently im-
pressed by the architecture of Celebration to further
check out the movement known as the New Urbanism, and what I found was refreshingly practical,
people-centered, and democratic. Sometimes called
"neo-traditional planning" or "traditional American
town making," the movement is predicated on the
age-old habits that all people, rich or poor, have historically exhibited in towns. Rejecting separate-use
and car-oriented zoning, the movement takes the concepts of urbanism Jane Jacobs described in *The Life and
Death of American Cities* out to suburbs and towns.
Championing walking, public transport, and the
mixed use of buildings by stores and residences, the
New Urbanism works to create towns and neighborhoods, unlike the business-oriented vision of planning that has created sprawl.

"Like the habitat of a species, the neighborhood
possesses a natural logic that can be described in
physical terms," Andres Duany and Elizabeth Plater-
Zyberk, the best known of the movement's adherents,
have written. They believe such a neighborhood generally has a public space at its center and a discernible
edge about one-quarter of a mile away; within it, different ages and types of people live, shop, work, learn,
and play. These ideas recall the European market
town or the New England town organized around a
green or commons. Indeed, New Urbanist planners
see the traditional town block as "a versatile, ancient

instrument . . . [that] allows a mutually beneficial re-
lationship of space and vehicles in urban space." But
most of all, the movement addresses people's emotional and human needs for community. Pedestrian
and public transit encourages more spontaneous in-
teractions between people, and allows children and
seniors, for instance, who might tend to be home-
bound in car-oriented developments, to participate
more fully and naturally in community life.

As traditional towns once took their form in relation to their natural surroundings, so New Urbanist
architects accept the physical constraints of mountain
and river and see trees as symbolic of our long inter-
action with nature, regarding even the suburb as a
natural environment rather than a tabula rasa on
which to scoop out, for instance, the fake lakes found
in Dallas, Las Vegas, and Kissimmee. They encourage
authentic regional building differences and energy-
efficient, nonpolluting construction. They believe
that buildings should be permanent, well-made fix-
tures of the landscape rather than products to be
consumed and discarded.

One of the most powerful arguments for the New
Urbanist agenda is demographic. The single-family
detached house with lawn and garage is designed for
married couples with children, a group that, according
to the 1990 census, now constitutes only 26 percent of
American households. Single-person households are
more common, making up 30 percent of the total;
families without children account for 36 percent, and
single parents with children the remaining 8 percent.
With double-income households now representing
more than half of all families, "women are certainly
less available to support a suburban family lifestyle

which requires a chauffeur for every child's trip,"
writes Peter Calthorpe, an architect and the author of
*The Next American Metropolis.* Moreover, as the critic
Thomas Fisher put it in *Progressive Architecture,*

> If we will have to live more frugally as high-wage jobs
> continue to disappear, if we have to depend more upon
> family and friends as job security becomes a thing of
> the past, if information highways and interactive com-
> puter and television networks turn the home into a
> place to work and shop as well as to live, then the new
> towns seem better suited to our needs than the old sub-
> urbs they seek to replace.

New Urbanist planning can serve a variety of situa-
tions. It is well suited to metropolitan areas where
land prices necessitate higher density, and to states
like Washington, whose cities restrict low-density
development. It can also be used in suburban infill
and redevelopment sites, particularly in places like
Portland, Oregon, which has an urban growth boundary and enough density for mass transit. Separate new
towns are the easiest to design with the pedestrian in
mind; they can be situated within transit reach of a
city center and can more easily afford greenbelts; there
will also be opportunities to redevelop large commercial spaces as the population continues to grow. But
the New Urbanism is not a quick panacea for growth
and sprawl. Departments of public works, boards
of education, and other official bodies must often be
convinced of the merits of its objectives: A school
board may require more land than can be comfortably
accommodated in a pedestrian-scale development,
or a street must be made private to make a pedestrian-
scale intersection feasible, with the cost passed on to
homeowners. Moreover, cities like Phoenix and Las

Vegas, which have allowed extended growth at a very
low density, will never have enough density to support pedestrian or public transit.

Some critics find the movement annoyingly un-
original, even a nostalgic flight from modernity, and
it is true that some developments, such as Kentlands,
look almost too historical, although Seaside, Florida,
and many other ventures do not. But the movement
never intended to be necessarily original. It is instead
a clearly articulated reaction to the profound sense of
placelessness and impersonality of much of American
development. It is a response to four decades of housing practices that have reinforced separate gender
roles, enjoined us to waste energy, enslaved us to the
automobile, deprived us of regional built culture,
and segregated us by age, race, class, and family pref-
erences. It is also a reaction to the pompous and
grandiose architecture of the savings and loan years,
to the visual chaos of strips and edge cities, to the
bunker mentality of gate-guarded communities, and
to the privatization of American life that has left us
with an indifference to democracy and the social good
reflected in our voting habits.

Indeed, with no apology the New Urbanism marks
a return to a classic and vernacular American planning
tradition that flourished in the 1910s and 1920s,
"to principles about building communities," architect
Todd Bressi believes, "that have been virtually ignored
for half a century." Including planners like Frederick
Law Olmsted Jr., Coral Gables, Florida developer
George Merrick, and City Beautiful planner John
Nolen, among many others, this tradition embraced
symbolic, strategically located public spaces, small
lots, and gridded streets, and it even succeeded with

public housing. A World War I housing shortage for munitions manufacturing workers encouraged Congress to approve $50 million and later $100 million in May 1918 to build emergency housing in Philadelphia, Washington, Newport News, Bridgeport, and elsewhere along the Eastern seaboard. Modest, economical, and still attractive today, the housing for factory workers in Bridgeport, for example, consists of brick row houses with slate roofs and dormers, designed in Colonial, Federal Revival, or Tudor Revival styles and laid out with forecourts, courtyards, and gently curving streets. Unfortunately for this early venture into public housing, 1919 marked the country's first great red scare. The workers' housing in Bridgeport was cited for "undue elegance in design," the architectural historian Vincent Scully recalls with irony. And soon congressional investigation was convened that discouraged such efforts. Regional and town planning along these classical lines continued, however, into the 1920s, with a regional plan for New York, a residential complex in Radburn, New Jersey, and many other projects, but the movement lost momentum when the depression devastated the construction industry. The Stamford that was demolished partook of many of these principles, leading to the discomfiting thought that if we had left our downtowns intact, they might once again have fitted our needs, as city centers in Europe have traditionally done.

The New Urbanism is a throwback in another way, too: If American housing trends have been toward privatization, this movement insists on a reassertion of government or civic power into the everyday landscape. Thomas Fisher sees the movement as reflecting reasoned argument, rule of law, and Enlightenment principles of democratic society. Although the idea that the community can exercise control over the appearance of one's property has evolved with the rise of historic districts, design review boards, and the covenants of traditional community-interest developments, the New Urbanism certainly goes against the current political climate that calls endlessly for a diminished government role. In seeking to be inclusive rather than exclusive, in resurrecting the idea that social classes can harmoniously live together in the right environments, the New Urbanism brings a sense of social mission to a profession that has been mired in what Fisher has called a "nihilistic individualism" that has scorned a social role for architects. The modernist ethos of aesthetic experimentation consigned many architects to the effete and exclusive role of designing for the rich, while the total failure of high-rise, low-income housing projects like Pruitt-Igoe in St. Louis and those in Newark and Chicago that had to be dynamited convinced many modernists that architectural efforts at social reform were destined to failure (though the New Urbanism might counter that these were flawed and inhuman designs). The New Urbanism, by contrast, has instilled in many architects a new sense of mission and social relevance. Indeed, the first meeting of the Congress of New Urbanism in 1993 has been described as having the feel of a crusade, and there is, indeed, a sense of moral urgency in the books and articles by New Urbanism planners and architects, in the imperatives of Peter Calthorpe that we should "help create communities, not sprawl . . . that we must return meaning and stature to the physical expressions of our public life."

But if New Urbanists seem fervent it is at least

partly the result of having attempted the daunting task of overthrowing the immense and dedicated machine of American tract suburbanization and of having met with some success. Since 1984, when Duany and Plater-Zyberk's Seaside, Florida, development attracted widespread acclaim, New Urbanist designs have come to form the majority of submissions for the *Progressive Architecture* Awards program; the appearance of its designs in upscale magazines like *Metropolitan Home* suggests its attraction to the young and upwardly mobile. And with projects in Sacramento and Culver City, California, Memphis, Tennessee, Alexandria, Virginia, Cleveland's inner city, and New York's Battery Park City, to name but a few, the movement can certainly be said to be having an impact. Unfortunately, the movement's residential developments, most successful as new towns, are being undertaken in the context of increased community-interest developments, rendering its commitment to democratic principles far more hamstrung than it would have been before the CID era.

Fundamentally, the reinforcement of the public sphere that the New Urbanism champions is really about that anachronistic-sounding concept called "civics," a subject that used to be, but of course is no longer, a staple of American public education. That Calthorpe's belief that "public spaces should provide the fundamental order of our communities and set the limits to our private domain" should sound "new" is a testament to how completely America has repressed its civic responsibilities. The word civics, after all, presupposes a vision of what a society grants and expects of its citizens, and such a vision is lacking in this country, which is concerned with allowing some people to make as much money as they please rather than with creating a responsible human society. What is also haunting and sad, in terms of American society, is that it was not until the fall of the Soviet Union and the 1990s that concepts such as community and civic life reentered the public discourse, an example of how even innocent and decent notions of community were demonized and denied us during the Cold War era.

# The Uses of Modernism

In the early decades of the twentieth century, the
American vernacular planning tradition predating the
New Urbanism was swept aside by the aesthetic of
modernism. Accepting mechanization, mass consumption, and incessant change as central and defin-
ing features of contemporary life, modernism affected
nearly all the arts. Modernists avoided age-old forms
such as representational painting, traditional narrative, and tonal music and instead sought untried
artistic strategies for the strange new world of the
twentieth century. In architecture, designs were often
technologically inspired; extolling the functional and
banishing ornamentation, architects created buildings
from industrial materials like concrete and steel. A
radical departure that eventually became the norm,
modernism presupposed not our similarities to previ-
ous generations but our differences from them, as if
our century were an apex or endpoint rather than another phase in a long continuum of history.

But consigning the past to the rubbish heap was ar-
rogant and destructive. As far as Vincent Scully was
concerned, "The Modern architects of the heroic
period (Wright, Le Corbusier, Mies van der Rohe,
Gropius and their followers) all despised the traditional city—the finest achievement of Western
architecture, put together piece by piece over the centuries—and were determined to replace it with their
own personal, idiosyncratic schemes." Modernism
held to an effete and romantic conception of the

architect as a leader uniquely capable of seeing what
the masses could not. In the fine arts, it engendered
the idea of art for art's sake, which downplayed the
concept that art should seek a direct emotional connection with its audience or serve moral or political
ends; in architecture and planning, it fostered an international and rational style dedicated more to social organization than to the emotional and aesthetic needs
of its users. By its relative indifference to the prefer-
ences of its audience, modernism directly or indirectly
encouraged the emerging idea of the mass man. Like
W. H. Auden's "Unknown Citizen" who "except for
the War till the day he retired/ . . . worked for a factory
and never got fired," the mass man was a person
whose life could be shaped by marketing experts, the
media, the architect, and the will of state, a being who
bowed to the overwhelming technological and bu-
reaucratic forces of the times, the archetypal worker,
consumer, or soldier rather than an individual.

The concept of the mass man gained momentum
as the century progressed, especially given the mobi-
lizations and exterminations of World War II. And
having moved large numbers of men to the front,
women to the factories, and Japanese Americans to
the internment camps, the postwar American government encouraged the rise of a mass consumer society.
The country's newfound prosperity, combined with
the moral victory over Hitler and the awesome power
of the atom bomb, seemed to justify mass projects
such as urban renewal and suburbanization, which expressed a modernist aesthetic of place. Indeed, during
the postwar period high modernism became deeply
entrenched; to oppose it, especially in the arts, was to
invite scorn. Much reference has been made to the

"canonical modernism" in postwar architecture, and
in classical music it took the form of atonal serialism,
whose proponents, one composer recalled, "presented
and still present it as the only true faith, an orthodox
cultural church . . . [that] quickly captured and dominated American academic circles, which it mon-
strously and bluntly politicized." Even as late as the
1970s I had to abandon plans for a college English major because, seeing literature as an essentially moral
activity, I could find no pleasure in writing about
the role of water in a Shakespeare play or that of the
candelabra in a Virginia Woolf novel, themes conso-
nant with the modernist "New Criticism" so heavy on
symbolism and light on social, historical, and moral
content.

The constraint to conform produced by modernism paralleled and reinforced similar pressures
exerted during the Cold War. Indeed, modernism's
influence went beyond countries and ideologies because it was a convenient screen for the consolidation
of power from above; modernist architecture appeared
in both capitalist and communist countries. During
the late 1960s, 1970s, and 1980s in the United States,
however, modernism became detached from the realm
of architects and artists and converted into a powerful
economic tool that developers used to create the suburban sprawl where most Americans live today. For it
simply doesn't make sense to ascribe our landscape's
overwhelming lack of ornamentation, orientation
around the car, and ahistorical focus solely to an aesthetic movement when these attributes so clearly help
developers in their favorite activity of lowering the bottom line. "The height, shape, size, density, orientation,
and materials of most buildings are largely determined

by the formulaic economics of the Deal," Joel Garreau described the priorities of the building industries after traveling the country for *Edge City*, his 1993 study of ex-urban development. Chain enterprises have saved money on design and increased customer recognition by making America look the same everywhere. The austere outer walls of "big box" stores and malls enable marketing dollars to be spent inside to persuade consumers already inside to stay longer and buy more. "Teardown" developments are examples of planned obsolescence, and consumerism's celebration of the new, aided by American racism, helped justify the abandonment of historic urban downtowns. As sprawl and corporate real estate interests consumed pieces of land here and there in an incremental process that took decades, we failed to comprehend—or to be able to stop—the degradation of the majestic and irreplaceable American landscape. And somehow its transformation was vaguely seen as a progression from the modernist ethos rather than the unprecedented physical entrenchment of corporate economic power that it was.

At the same time, government's role in protecting us from the cynical calculations of the market has weakened. Activities once seen as government's exclusive domain, such as welfare, education, and corrections, are being increasingly given over to the private sector. And a capitalist ethos has crept into government's own conception of itself: If a for-profit body finds education and preventive medicine and the arts expendable overhead, government should too. Two decades of government belt-tightening and increasing corporate control have left our societal expectations, to use the appropriate language, downsized, a state of

affairs that is unquestionably convenient for corporate
interests. Convenient too, is the fact that, perhaps because consumerism tends to rivet our attention to our
individual desires, a sense of civic responsibility fails
to occupy a central part of our consciousness; less
than half the Americans able to do so vote. But even
with a downsized government, voluntary participation, and one of the lowest tax rates in the industrialized world, we constantly hear reports of the
American people's anger at "big government" and
taxation. Unlike consumerism, taxation, an expression of the idea that in addition to being individual
citizens we are also part of a whole, calls upon social
and communal skills. But just as the doctrine of
Manifest Destiny helped justify a huge land grab on
the basis of race, just as modernism and "growth"
helped justify the really ugly and wasteful treatment
of the American landscape, antitax rhetoric helps justify the diminishing role of government and the rising
power and influence of the private sector. Moroever,
that the twentieth century's last great imperial conflict, the Cold War between the Soviet Union and the
United States, was won not by government troops but
by the market economy may also suggest that we are
passing from an era in which nation-states prevailed
to one in which economic forces will.

The disparity in income between rich and poor
Americans that had started me on my journey continued to grow, the Census Bureau reported in June 1996.
Now using more detailed reporting techniques and
computers, the Bureau found the gap wider than
had been previously estimated; observers noted its
increasing entrenchment as a feature of the economy.

I wasn't particularly surprised because my travels had made clear that the private sector encourages the stratification of class. Still, it was depressing to read that in the three years ending in April 1997, low-paying, no-frills service-related jobs were created at *22 times* the rate of high-wage jobs with benefits. I hoped that we would not sit idly by as disparity became a fixture of our lives, the way we had watched as the commercialization of the landscape became permanent. But we might easily do so. After all, the private sector, ever planning new products, is oriented toward the future. Consumers waiting to be sold them, however, live in the present. Both modernism *and* capitalism advocate a mental abolition of the past that inflates the strength and importance of the immediate, material reality. We might forget that there ever *was* a moment of less disparity.

The past reminds us of timeless human truths and allows for the perpetuation of cultural traditions that can be nourishing; it contains examples of mistakes to avoid, preserves the memory of alternative ways of doing things, and is the basis for self-understanding upon which all psychotherapies depend. Its presence gives us more insight when making choices; its lack allows myth to flourish and rhetoric to enter the void. "A city without an old town is like a shell without a pearl," the European writer Slavenka Drakulic has written; cities put together over the centuries are our physical embodiments of the past. They are places in which to consider the cumulative work of the species, to connect with both dead and living humanity, to see what creations the dead left for us while they were here in this place we now inhabit. Like any other, our country had a built past that could have endured, but we have lost the possibility of experiencing it in city after city and town after town. Did we really want to treat the things the dead left for us, or even ourselves, this way? Can we really pretend that we have *chosen* this?

This country was created out of an Englightenment vision in which the rights of human beings, even if at the time only of *some* human beings, were paramount. This fundamentally moral and humanistic vision should remind us that there are values other than economic ones with which to shape our country. One need only think of the 400-year Atlantic slave trade or the exploits of the big tobacco companies to know that the directions in which commerce heads are not always toward higher purposes. "Growth for the sake of growth," the writer Edward Abbey reminds us, "is the ideology of the cancer cell."

# Notes

Because I believe the stories, rather than the individual players, are paramount, I have not generally named the people I interviewed; unless otherwise specified, all quotations from local residents, officials, and others are from interviews I held with them during my visits: to Stamford, December and January 1993–1994; to Hilton Head, January 6–11, 1996; to Branson, August 10–15, 1994; to Dallas, March 21–28, 1993; to Simi Valley, March 18–24, 1996; to Las Vegas, November 1992; to Celebration, June 3–6, 1997.

### An Unusual Motivation

The statistics and quotation on wealth concentration are from Sylvia Nasar, "Fed Gives New Evidence of 80's Gain by Richest," *The New York Times*, April 21, 1992, p. 1. The quotation about the value of the past to the real estate industry is from Joel Barna, *The See-Through Years* (Rice University Press, 1993), p. 28. Neil Postman on children is from *The Disappearance of Childhood* (Delacorte Press, 1982), p. 1. Lewis Lapham's remarks are from his essay "Robber Barons Redux" in *Harper's* (January 1994), p. 11. The information that Americans tripled the amount they spent gambling in a decade is from Peter Applebome, "Casino Boom along Gulf Coast," *The New York Times*, January 10, 1994, p. A1. The statistic on the average CEO's salary comes from Andrew Hacker's *Money* (Scribner, 1997), p. 53.

### New City

The government center's purchase from GTE before the market collapsed was recounted to me by city officials, the art preservationist, and others, in December 1993. On the early history of Stamford, see E. Feinstein, *Stamford from Puritan to Patriot* and E. Bronson, ed., *Stamford: Past and Present,*

*1641– 1976* (Stamford Bicentennial Committee, 1976);
E. Feinstein, *Stamford in the Gilded Age* (Stamford Historical
Society, 1973); E. Feinstein and J. Pendry, *Stamford: An Illus-
trated History* (Windsor, 1984); E. B. Huntington, *History of
Stamford* (Harbor Hill Books, 1979); and H. F. Sherwood, *Story
of Stamford* (States History Company, 1930). The approxi-
mate sales price of improved urban renewal land is from
Martin Anderson, *The Federal Bulldozer* (MIT Press, 1964),
pp. 21–22. On 94 percent of Southeast Quadrant housing as
substandard and downtown flooding, see "Seven Years to
Success: A Special CAC Report to Stamford Citizens on Urban
Renewal," *Stamford Advocate*, January 8, 1963, p. 5. For the
many individual shops in earlier eras, see old atlases in the
Stamford Government Center. On downtown Stamford as
a "dying body" and the inner loop highway, see "Seven
Years," p. 6. On the makeup of the Executive Committee of
the Citizens' Action Council, see "Seven Years," p. 8. The
psychological study on Boston's West End is by Marc Fried,
"Grieving for a Lost Home: Psychological Costs of Relocation," in James Q. Wilson (ed.), *Urban Renewal: The Record
and the Controversy* (MIT Press, 1966), pp. 359–379, esp. p. 360.
On Stamford trailing only New York and Chicago in numbers
of corporate headquarters, see T. Lueck, "An Office Boom
Transforms Once-Ailing Connecticut City," *The New York
Times*, March 10, 1985, p. 1. For the variances granted in ex-
change for public amenities and their advertising, see Merci
Federici, "Stamford's Amenity Bonus Program," unpublished
paper, Stamford Area Studies, University of Connecticut,
April 1989, collection of Renee Kahn. On the mall as "mega-
structure," see Paul Goldberger, "Stamford's Renewal: Sun
Belt in Connecticut," *The New York Times*, March 11, 1985,
p. 1. "The Great Wall" and "Fort Stamford" were common
expressions. The quotation on territorial attachments in the
global age is from Richard J. Barnet and John Cavanaugh,
*Global Dreams: Imperial Corporations and the New World Order*
(Simon and Schuster, 1994), p. 19. The quotation from
William H. Whyte is used by permission. Vincent Scully on
buildings and social values is from Eleanor Charles, "Society
Will Build What It Believes In," *The New York Times* (Connecticut section), February 7, 1988, sec. 11, p. 3.

## Privatopia

For general information on CIDs, see Stephen E. Barton and Carol Silverman, *Common Interest Communities: Private Governments and the Public Interest* (Institute of Governmental Studies Press, University of California, 1994), and Evan McKenzie, *Privatopia* (Yale University Press, 1994). On the history of CIDs, see McKenzie, esp. pp. 39–43. For Worley's words see *J. C. Nichols and the Shaping of Kansas City* (University of Missouri Press, 1990), pp. 167–68. The following refer to McKenzie: on the domination of corporate builders, pp. 80–81; on the comparative cost of land to building, Martin Mayer, quoted on p. 83; on the "new towns," p. 100; on FHA approval of "cluster subdivisions," p. 85; for the quotation on the industry grabbing the idea, p. 93; on the nationwide growth and comparative numbers of CIDs, p. 11; on the writing of CC&Rs by developers, p. 127; on developers retaining three votes per unsold unit, p. 128; for Adolph Berle's remarks, p. 135. Grant McConnell's thoughts can be found in *Private Power and American Democracy* (Knopf, 1966), esp. chapter 5. The following refer to McKenzie: on changing CCRs and the disenfranchisement of renters, pp. 127, 128; for the quotation on subservience to the corporation, p. 142; on consent and availability of non-CID housing, p. 147; Robert Reich is quoted on pp. 186 and 175; Charles Murray is quoted on p. 175 and summarized on p. 23; for industry estimates on 225,000 associations by the year 2000 p.11; the figure of 48 million people in those 225,000 associations is my own estimate based on McKenzie's figures that 32 million lived under 150,000 associations in 1992.

## The Coastal Empire

The hodgepodge quotation is found in Michael Danielson, *Profits and Politics in Paradise: The Development of Hilton Head Island* (University of South Carolina Press, 1995), p. 24; for "high-quality destination resort" and income of Sea Pines residents, see p. 102; on the general history of the island, pp. 7–8. On Columbus's adventures in slave-trading see Hugh Thomas, *The Slave Trade* (Simon & Schuster, 1997), p. 89. On

South Carolina's founding by white Barbadians, see Peter H.
Wood, *Black Majority: Negroes in Colonial South Carolina from
1670 to the Stono Rebellion* (Knopf, 1974), chapter 1; for African knowledge of cultivation of rice, pp. 59–62. For blacks
outnumbering whites, see ibid., passim, and John Lofton,
*Denmark Vesey's Revolt* (Kent State University Press, 1983),
pp. 38–39. On the slave code's origins in Barbados, see
Lofton, p. 43. For Union forces on Hilton Head, see *Mitchelville: Experiment in Freedom* (Chicora Foundation, 1995),
p. 1; on Lincoln's freeing of the Sea Island slaves, p. 3; on
Mitchelville as first site of compulsory education and other
details, pp. 4–6; on U.S. government control of land, p. 8.
On the Freedman's Bureau Act of 1866, see G. P. Sanger, ed.,
*United States Statutes at Large*, vol. 14, p. 175. For Andrew
Johnson's evil deeds, see Eric L. McKitrick, *Andrew Johnson
and Reconstruction* (University of Chicago Press, 1960), esp.
chapters 1 and 10. On parcels sold to freedmen and black
speculators, see *Mitchelville*, p. 8. On the Southern Homestead Act, see M. Lanza, *Agrarianism and Reconstruction Politics* (Louisiana State University Press, 1990), esp. p. 141. On
native owners and Roy Rainey, see Danielson, p. 6, and
*Mitchelville*, p. 10. For "ripe for development," see Danielson,
p. 6. On education and freedom of the mails and expression,
see Clement Eaton, *Freedom of Thought in the Old South* (Duke
University Press, 1940), esp. chapters 3, 7, and 8. On the cultural mores of the Charleston elite, see George C. Rogers,
*Charleston in the Age of the Pinckneys* (University of Oklahoma Press, 1969), esp. pp. 72–73, 99–101, and chapter 6. On
the term *contraband*, see David Herbert Donald, *Lincoln* (Simon and Schuster, 1995), p. 343, and *Mitchelville*, p. 3. The
quotation about the American slave system is from Orlando
Patterson, *Slavery and Social Death* (Harvard University Press,
1982), p. 76; on manumission, see esp. pp. 286 and 245, and
chapters 8, 9, and 10. The conclusion that there was no
moral reeducation is the result of my own reading and is sec-
onded by historian John Blassingame of Yale University. The
quotation about tribes is from Danielson, p. 115. On "stack-
a-shacks" and later Hilton Head development, see also
Danielson, pp. 164, 178, and passim. The quotation on zoning

as a chief instrument is from David Kirp et al., *Our Town: Race, Housing, and the Soul of Suburbia* (Rutgers University Press, 1995), p. 8. The black population numbers vary. *Mitchelville*, p. 10, reports nearly 3,000 in 1980 and 300 in late 1930s; Danielson, p. 11, cites 1,000 in the mid-twentieth century. On NAACP legal challenges, see Town of Hilton Head files on incorporation; also Danielson, p. 183. The remarks from the R/UDAT study are from American Institute of Architects, *Hilton Head Island R/UDAT*, October 5–9, 1995, pp. 4, 54, 55. The Princeton expert cited is Danielson, p. 286. On the thematic travel center see *Hilton Head News*, January 10, 1996, p. B2. For Lincoln's words on the people's contest, see Donald, p. 304. The final quotations of the piece, of course, are from Lincoln's Gettysburg Address.

### Entertainment Capitals

The demolition of the old Orlando city hall was the talk of the town and front-page news when I visited Disney World to write my article "Heaven's Place: Report from Central Florida," which appeared in the *Threepenny Review*, December 1992 and which also reports the incident. For the figure that shows amusement and recreation revenues increasing from $12.4 billion in 1980 to $24 billion in 1987, see Bureau of Statistics, Treasury Department. *Statistical Abstract of the United States* (Washington: GPO, 1990), table 1381.

### Hub of the Hinterlands

Although rhetorically slanted, Branson promotional material contains an excellent supply of local lore. My history of Branson comes from *Ozark Trails Magazine* (Summer/Fall 1994), and the historical articles on pp. 21–29 of *Branson Encore* Souvenir Magazine (copyright 1993, Branson Encore Publishing). The mention of Harold Bell Wright as a ridiculed writer is from Lawrence Tagg, *Harold Bell Wright* (Westernlore Press, 1986), chapter 5; on Wright's sales, see p. 53. On "creative level" see Peter Applebome, "Miles from Anywhere, Flocks of Tourists Descend," *The New York Times*,

June 1, 1993, p. 10. On Wright's life see Tagg, pp. 28–51; on the marketing of his book, p. 57. The *Branson Belle* was launched on August 12, 1994, when I was in town, and the information on its fueling comes from its public relations office. The description of corporate interest in Branson is from an article in E. McDowell, "Expansion in a Country Music Town," *The New York Times*, June 17, 1993, p. 10.

*Free-for-All*

The main sources used here are Michael Waldman, *Who Robbed America? A Citizen's Guide to the Savings and Loan Scandal* (Random House, 1990); Stephen Pizzo, Mary Fricker, and Paul Muolo, *Inside Job* (McGraw-Hill, 1989); and Paul Zane Pilzer with Robert Dietz, *Other Peoples' Money* (Simon and Schuster, 1989). Of these, Pizzo, et al. is the most authoritative. For the beginnings of S&Ls and their history through the depression, see Pizzo, et al., pp. 9–11, esp. p. 10 for "fuel for the home-building engine"; and Pilzer, pp. 14, 33; the quotations about confidence and about not needing to be a genius are from ibid., pp. 67 and 70. Ronald Reagan's jackpot quotation is from Pizzo, et al., p. 2, and the explanation of Garn-St. Germain is largely from ibid., pp. 12–13. On Charles Keating and the five senators, see Pizzo, et al., pp. 392–404; for Ed Gray's relationships with Donald Regan and S&L owners, see pp. 16, 78–79; on Ed Gray as a "Nazi," p. 211; for how much was on hand to cover deposits, p. 213. On Gray's efforts to cut losses, see Pizzo, et al., pp. 105–106; on the S&L-Bush connection, see Pizzo, et al., pp. 250, 313–314, Pilzer, p. 209, and Waldman, pp. 138, 141, 143, and 189. On the FDIC chairman's remarks on the RTC, see Pizzo, et al., p. 250. On California, see Pilzer, pp. 124–133; the numbers on Texas and California thrifts are from Resolution Trust Corporation Thrift Financial Report, December 31, 1989, quoted in Waldman, p. 230. On developers in Texas S&Ls, see Pizzo, et al., p. 20. The quotation on Texas buy-and-flip closings is from ibid., p. 207; the statistics on Vernon's bad loans are from Pilzer, p. 88.

## Reflections in a Mirror-Skin Building

The number of housing units in downtown Dallas is from interviews with city officials and preservationists, April 1993; David Dillon, *Dallas Architecture, 1936–1986* (Texas Monthly Press, 1985), p. 79, describes the downtown as having "no housing." On the downtown's 9 to 5 nature, see Dillon, p. 167. The source for Dallas's vacancy rates is Jeanne B. Pinder, "Downtown's Empty Feeling," *The New York Times,* May 9, 1993, sec. 3, p. 5. The figures on the companies coming to Dallas because of the airport and business climate are from the booklet *Alliance* (Perot Group, 1993). The history of Dallas comes from a variety of sources, most notably Dillon, pp. 1, 2, 67, 119, 151, and passim. That half of the downtown buildings were destroyed is from interviews and Dillon, pp. 67, 68, 76, 79, and 95. That development proceeded northward and that Oak Cliff threatened to secede is common knowledge in Dallas, and was told to me in interviews with architects and planners and confirmed by street signs urging secession in Oak Cliff. On Las Colinas, see Joel Barna, *The See-Through Years* (Rice University Press, 1993), pp. 38–41, Dillon, pp. 151, 178–181, and the Las Colinas marketing packet; the remarks from the marketing man are from an interview with the author, April 1993. On the history of two-tiered cities, see Trevor Boddy, "Underground and Overhead: Building the Analogous City," in M. Sorkin (ed.), *Variations on a Theme Park* (Hill and Wang, 1992), pp. 127–36; the quotation on the "middle-class tyranny" is from p. 150. On the concept of developers as princes, see Barna, p. 21. The figure of 45 percent occupancy of the Providence Towers is from a telephone interview with the Towers' management company, May 1993. The concept of using the landscape as a blank canvas for marketing ideas is from Barna in correspondence to the author, 1993. On the razing of houses in Vineyard and elsewhere, see Barna, p. 245, Dillon, p. 117, or the sites themselves. Other information on Southland was obtained from interviews with city officials and the head of the Dallas Plan, April 1993. On Robert Folsom's Bent Tree office towers, see Darrell Preston, "From Debtors to Deal Makers: After Defaulting on Millions, Developers Still Cut Deals with

BETTINA DREW

Feds," *Dallas Business Journal*, May 28, 1993, p. 1, and Dillon, p. 129. On the development that took off in 1976, see Dillon, pp. 117, 128–130, 147, and 186. On savings and loan thieves picking up bargain properties, see Preston. The information concerning the history of Alliance Airport came from an interview with Alliance marketing, April 1993; see also their promotional packets. On Ross Jr.'s lobbying the Texas legislature, Jim Wright's participation in Alliance, and government support for the project, see Dean Baquet, "Perot Investments in Land Thrive with Public Funds," *The New York Times*, May 29, 1992, p. 1 and Elaine Buckberg, "Airport '89: Welfare for H. Ross Perot," *The New Republic*, August 21, 1989, p. 12. The quotation on the paternalism of the corporate developments is from Barna, p. 195. On the construction of the highway linking Alliance to DFW, see the Perot Group, Baquet, "Perot Investments," and Elaine Buckberg, "Airport '89."

*A Clouding Over of the Blue-Sky Dream*

On the railroad coming to southern California and land sales there, see J. Cameron, *Simi Grows Up* (Simi Valley Historical Society, 1963), p. 27; on the land and water companies and blacksnake whips, see pp. 28–30. The 150 bad-air days and the Bank of America study are cited in Timothy Egan's excellent "Urban Sprawl Strains Western States," *The New York Times*, December 29, 1996, pp. 1 and 20. For statistics on job loss and immigration, see Stryker McGuire and Andrew Muir, "California in the Rear-view Mirror," *Newsweek*, July 19, 1993. The statistics on the American Farmland Trust were quoted in Carey Goldberg, "Alarm Bells Sounding as Suburbs Gobble Up California's Richest Farmland," *The New York Times*, June 20, 1996, p. 1.

*In the Red Rock Valley of the Cowboy Westerns*

The opening quotation from Ronald Reagan was on display at the Ronald Reagan Museum when I visited it in March 1996. The history of the post-1960s development of the valley is from interviews, *Simi Grows Up*, and exhibits at the Simi Valley Historical Society. The phrase "valley of your future" is from promotional brochures in the collection of the historical society. That it was possible to buy a house with the GI Bill and five hundred dollars or nothing down was told to me in a number of interviews with long-time residents, in particular one at the city planning office and the other at the historical society. The figures on Simi's population growth are from an exhibit at the historical society, March 1996; the statements on who it attracted were confirmed over and over in interviews. The details on the creation of local government were recounted to me by the long-term resident in the city planning office cited above. The survey which elicited the numerous quotations, entitled "20/20," was made available to me by the City of Simi Valley. The city official mentioning the LAPD was one of several. The phrase "trashy and cluttered" is from the survey. That crime was down was confirmed to me by both city officials and a spokesperson for the SVPD. The quotes from teenagers about the police are from a group of seniors that I spoke to at Simi Valley High School. The parties were described to me by a guidance counselor at Simi Valley High, who introduced me to a party host and other students who confirmed their regularity. The average Simi Valley home price (as of March 1996) was provided to me by the Simi Valley Association of Realtors. The information on the first trial of the LAPD officers and its aftermath in Simi Valley is a synthesis of news clippings made available to me by the *Simi Valley Star* and the Simi Valley Historical Society, as well as information from interviews with city officials and workers. The closing of the GM plant is part of the local memory. The information on the earthquake is from the newspaper clipping collection of the Simi Valley Historical Society. The quotations on the frontier myth are from Richard Slotkin, *Gunfighter Nation* (HarperPerennial, 1992), pp. 11–16. On the nineteenth-century idea of the Anglo-Saxon race, see Reginald Horsman, *Race and Manifest Destiny* (Harvard University Press, 1981). For the quotation on history as psychiatric service, see Patricia Limerick, "The Canon Debate from a Historian's Perpsective," *Journal of Legal Education* (March 1993), p. 6.

BETTINA DREW

*Living on the Highway*

The opening description of the Mall of America is from
David Guterson, "Enclosed. Encyclopedic. Endured: The
Mall of America," in Peterson et al., *The Norton Reader*, 9th
ed. (Norton, 1996), p. 210. The statistic about suburban
office space is from Joel Garreau, *Edge City* (Anchor Press,
1991), p. 5; see also Peter Calthorpe (ed.), *The Next American
Metropolis: Ecology, Community and the American Dream*
(Princeton Architectural Press, 1993), p. 19. The quotation
from James Howard Kuntsler, *Geography of Nowhere* (Simon
and Schuster, 1993), is on p. 131. The statistics on urban
population in the West, on vehicles miles traveled and the
quotations from Utah governor Leavitt and the Phoenix
antisprawl activist are from Timothy Egan, "Urban Sprawl
Strains Western States," in *The New York Times*, December 29,
1996, pp. 1 and 20; on vehicle miles see also Calthorpe, *Next
American Metropolis*, p. 27. The quotation on Denver's afternoon sun is from "Colorado's Front Range" in *National Geographic* (November 1996), p. 101. On Portland's urban
boundary, see Egan, "Drawing a Hard Line against Sprawl,"
*The New York Times*, December 30, 1966, pp. 1 and A12, and
Jay Walljasper, "Portland and Urban Planning," *The Nation*,
October 13, 1997. For details on the boundaries of other
cities mentioned, see Egan, "Drawing a Hard Line." The information on wildlife in Colorado is from "Colorado's Front
Range," pp. 86, 100; the quotation from Governor Romer is
on p. 100. The statistics on rural land lost to development
each year are from the American Farmland Trust, 1996.

*Please Play the Machines While You Wait*

On Las Vegas as the fastest-growing city of the 1980s, see
Timothy Egan, "Urban Sprawl Strains Western States," as
above. That more than 90 percent of the people have cars in
Las Vegas is from 1990 census statistics provided by the City
of Las Vegas. My little history of Las Vegas is distilled largely
from John Findlay, *People of Chance* (Oxford University
Press, 1986), from which comes the Bret Harte quotation
(p. 103) and the Erle Stanley Gardner quotation (p. 129).

*216*

That "multitudes of men were ready to lose their shirts" is from a letter from Roger Groening to the author, December 1992. For Las Vegas's development along the strip, see Findlay, chapter 5. The idea that the strip forced up the price of property is obvious, but was confirmed by the city planning department. The quotation from Nelson Algren is from *The Man with the Golden Arm* (Doubleday, 1949), p. 115. On the mob's cession of Las Vegas to the corporations, see David Johnston, *Temples of Chance: How America Inc., Bought Out Murder, Inc., to Win Control of the Casino Business* (Doubleday, 1992). My numbers on compulsive gamblers are from Gamblers Anonymous, 1993. On the accommodations Las Vegans have made to gambling, see Findlay, pp. 172 and 171–199. City and county officials told me of the water moratorium; on its suspension, see Egan, ibid. The information on mass transit was given to me in interviews with the planning office of the City of Las Vegas. On the pollution levels in Las Vegas, see Egan. "Mississippi West" was a term I heard repeatedly in interviews; Findlay discusses the long-standing segregation of blacks, pp. 189– 191. On the post L.A. riot violence and conditions on the West Side, see "Glitter Hides Seething Racial Tensions," *Los Angeles Times*, May 27, 1992, p. 1. The facts and figures about Summerlin are from the development's press and information packet, 1992. Andres Duany and Elizabeth Plater-Zyberk are quoted in William Schneider, "The Suburban Century Begins," *The Atlantic* (July 1992), p. 33. The statistics and occupancy rates for Excalibur as of late 1992 are from its public relations office. Marc Cooper's remarks are from his article "Fear and Lava," in the *Village Voice* (November 30, 1993), p. 38. Johnston's remarks about casino earnings are from *Temples*, p. 13. On the amounts Americans spent on gambling, see Peter Applebome, "Casino Boom Along Gulf Coast," *The New York Times*, January 10, 1994, p. 1.

*Déjà Vu*

The details on the white flight that open this chapter can be found in Timothy Egan, "Eastward Ho! The Great Move Reverses," *The New York Times*, January 31, 1996, pp. 1 and

20. The former mayor of Castle Rock's remarks are from Timothy Egan's "Urban Sprawl," pp. 1 and 20. On the U.S. government's supply of water to the Western states, Las Vegas's promise of water, the antigovernment attitudes of Westerners, the ensuing quotation, and the remarks of fomer Albuquerque mayor David Rusk, see Egan, ibid. For more on water in the West, see Charles Wilkinson, *Crossing the Next Meridian: Land, Water, and the Future of the West* (Island Press, 1992).

## *Celebration: A New Kind of American Town*

On the scope and price of the Capital Cities/ABC merger and 1994 setbacks, see Bernard Weinraub, "For Chairman, Deal Quenches Personal Thirst," *The New York Times*, August 1, 1995, p. 1. On Peter Rummell's and Eisner's remarks see *Celebration Chronicle* (Summer 1995), pp. 1 and 2. On reaching 99 percent of American homes, see "Media Monopoly Makers," *Multinational Monitor* (September 1995), p. 7. For the short history on Disney from 1964 to the 1980s, see Bettina Drew, "Heaven's Place: Report from Central Florida," *The Threepenny Review* (December 1992). On the cornerstones of Celebration, see *Celebration Chronicle* (Summer 1995), p. 2. On the lottery for Celebration, see Carol Lawson, "When You Wish upon a House," *The New York Times*, November 16, 1995, p. C1. On the Teaching Academy, see "Celebration, Florida Fact Sheet," Celebration Company, October 13, 1995. For the numbers of houses, I counted off the Celebration site plan. For Disney's words on EPCOT, see Michael Harrington, "To the Disney Station," *Harper's* (January 1979), pp. 35–139. For Eisner's remarks on Celebration, see *Celebration Chronicle* (Summer 1995), pp. 1 and 2. On Plater-Zyberk and Duany's codes, I rely on an interview with Vincent Scully, May 1997; for the characterization of their language, see Thomas Fisher, "Do the Suburbs Have a Future?" in *Progressive Architecture* (December 1993), p. 41. For details of Disney management inside Disney World, see The Project on Disney, *Inside the Mouse* (Duke University Press, 1995), esp. pp. 110–162; about "on" and "off" property, pp.113–114; on the suicide,

p. 115; on spying, p. 124; on corporate logic and control, p. 127. On nonparticipatory CID culture, see Barton and Silverman, chapter 6 and passim. On Celeration infrastructure government cannot afford, see *Celebration Chronicle* (Summer 1995), p. 11. Robert Stern's words are from a telephone interview, November 19, 1996. On the ranking of Florida schools, see National Center for Education Statistics, *Digest of Education Statistics* (GPO, 1996), p. 76 and the National Education Association, *Ranking of the States* (National Education Association, 1993), pp. 57–61; on Florida schoolchildren in Celebration, see Donna Young, "Celebration School Prepares to Transfer Out-of-Towners," *Orlando Business Journal*, March 27, 1998, p. 3. On the three-member board, see "Celebration, Florida Fact Sheet." For the little biography of Disney I have relied on Richard Schickel, *Disney Version* (Simon and Schuster, 1995), Marc Eliot, *Walt Disney: Hollywood's Dark Prince* (Carol, 1993), Eric Smoodin, *Disney Discourse* (Routledge, 1984), Leonard Maltin, *Disney Films* (Crown, 1984), Bob Thomas, *Walt Disney: An American Original* (Simon & Schuster, 1976), and Michael Harrington, "To the Disney Station." On *Song of the South*, see Mike Wallace, *Mickey Mouse History and Other Essays on American Memory* (Temple University Press, 1996), p. 36. Disneyland's discovery of the area's black and brown young people was reported on NPR's *All Things Considered* in the days following the riots. The analysis of Disney World exhibits is from Drew, "Heaven's Place." Robert Stone's remarks are taken from an interview with the author, September 1997. On books killed by publishers, see John Wiener, "Murdered Ink," *The Nation* (March 1993), p. 743. On Disney dealings with writers see Alan Bryman's introduction to his book *Disney and His Worlds* (Routledge, 1995). Statistics on foreign workers laboring on Disney products are from *U.S. in Haiti* (report from the National Labor Committee [NLC] Education Fund, January 1996); see also Barry Bearak, "Stitching Together a Crusade," *Los Angeles Times*, July 25, 1996; see also NLC press release, "Scores of Events Planned to Protest Ties to Sweatshops," (December 8, 1996), p. 1. Kernaghen's quotations are from an open letter to Michael Eisner from the NLC, May 26,

1996, p. 7. That Disney declined to meet, see December 8, 1996, NLC press release. On Eisner's salary, see NLC, *U.S. in Haiti*, p. 19. On Disney operations in Myanmar and China, see NLC, December 8, 1996 press release. On Capital Cities/ABC merger as second largest in U.S. history, making Disney the mightiest entertainment company on earth, see "Media Monopoly Makers," p. 7.

### The New Urbanism

The first quotation is from Andres Duany and Elizabeth Plater-Zyberk, "Neighborhood, District, and Corridor," in Peter Calthorpe (ed.), *The Next American Metropolis: Ecology, Community and the American Dream* (Princeton Architectural Press, 1993), p. xvii. The quotation about blocks is from Elizabeth Moule and Stefanos Polyzoides, "The Street, the Block, and the Building," ibid., p. xxii. The numbers from the census I found in Peter Katz's collection *The New Urbanism: Toward an Architecture of Community* (McGraw-Hill, 1994), p. 18; the quotation about women also can be found on p. 18. For the quotation about living more frugally, see Thomas Fisher, in "Do the Suburbs Have a Future?" in *Progressive Architecture* (December 1993), p. 41. The quote and thoughts on the old city-planning tradition are from Todd Bressi's essay "Planning the American Dream," in Katz, p. xxv. Professor Vincent Scully of Yale University provided me with information on the World War I housing for munitions workers, some of which I saw in Bridgeport; see also "Two Villages, Two Worlds," in *Progressive Architecture* (December 1993), pp. 50–53. For Fisher's thoughts on New Urbanism and democratic principles and his quotation on "nihilistic individualism," see "Do the Suburbs Have a Future?" *Progressive Architecture* (December 1993), p. 38. The quotations from Peter Calthorpe are from *Next American Metropolis*, pp. 17 and 23.

## *The Uses of Modernism*

The quotation from Vincent Scully is from his afterword, "The Architecture of Community," in Peter Katz's collection, *The New Urbanism: Toward an Architecture of Community* (McGraw-Hill, 1994), p. 223. The composer's remarks on atonal serialism in music are from Robert Schwarz, "In Contemporary Music: A House Still Divided," *The New York Times*, August 3, 1997, sec. 2, p. 24. The quotation from Joel Garreau is from *Edge City* (Anchor Press, 1991), p. 220. For the Census Bureau's findings on the disparity of incomes in the United States, see Stephen A. Holmes, "Income Disparity Between Richest and Poorest Rises," *The New York Times*, June 20, 1996, sec. A, p. 1. For the statistics on job creation in the three years before April 1997 and current bankruptcies, see Peter T. Kilborn, "Illness Is Turning into Financial Catastrophe for More of the Uninsured," *The New York Times*, August 1, 1997, sec. A, p. 10. The quotation from Drakulic is from "On the Quality of Wall Paint in Eastern Europe" in *How We Survived Communism and Even Laughed* (Hutchinson, 1987), p. 167. Edward Abbey is quoted in William Kittredge, "The Wild West's Not So-Natural Disasters," *The New York Times*, January 10, 1997, p. 33.

BETTINA DREW is the author of the critically acclaimed biography *Nelson Algren: A Life on the Wild Side* and the editor of *The Texas Stories of Nelson Algren.* Her essays have appeared in the *Yale Review*, the *Threepenny Review*, the *Chicago Tribune Sunday Magazine*, and other journals, and have been cited in *Best American Essays* 1992 and 1996 and nominated for Pushcart Prizes. She is the recipient of a Fellowship in Non-Fiction Literature from the New York Foundation on the Arts, and has taught English and American Studies at Yale University.

This book was designed by Will Powers. It is set in Stone Sans and Stone Serif typefaces by Stanton Publication Services, Inc., and manufactured by BookCrafters on acid-free paper.